Accessible Vacations

Accessible Vacations

An Insider's Guide to 10 National Parks

Simon J. Hayhoe

Rowman & Littlefield
Lanham • Boulder • New York • London

Published by Rowman & Littlefield
An imprint of The Rowman & Littlefield Publishing Group, Inc.
4501 Forbes Boulevard, Suite 200, Lanham, Maryland 20706
www.rowman.com

86-90 Paul Street, London EC2A 4NE, United Kingdom

British Library Cataloguing in Publication Information Available

Library of Congress Cataloging-in-Publication Data

Names: Hayhoe, Simon, author.
Title: Accessible vacations : an insider's guide to 10 national parks / Simon J. Hayhoe.
Description: Lanham, Maryland : Rowman & Littlefield, 2022. | Includes bibliographical references and index.
Identifiers: LCCN 2021042843 (print) | LCCN 2021042844 (ebook) | ISBN 9781538128671 (cloth) | ISBN 9781538128688 (epub)
Subjects: LCSH: People with disabilities—Travel—United States—Guidebooks. | National parks and reserves—United States—Guidebooks. | Parks—Barrier-free design.
Classification: LCC E160 .H38 2022 (print) | LCC E160 (ebook) | DDC 363.6/8087—dc23
LC record available at https://lccn.loc.gov/2021042843
LC ebook record available at https://lccn.loc.gov/2021042844

♾️™ The paper used in this publication meets the minimum requirements of American National Standard for Information Sciences—Permanence of Paper for Printed Library Materials, ANSI/NISO Z39.48-1992.

In memory of Margaret Ann Hayhoe,
with whom I enjoyed traveling

CONTENTS

CONTENTS

ACKNOWLEDGMENTS

I would like to thank the employees of the National Parks Service who provided information for this book and helped with the research. As they must remain anonymous, I can't thank them personally, but they know who they are. The five-step model was developed within the framework of the H2020 project ARCHES (http://www.ARCHES-project.eu), which has received funding from the European Union's Horizon 2020 research and innovation program under grant agreement no. 693229. In addition, I would like to acknowledge John Catt for helping with the chapter on inclusive technology.

PREFACE

I f you're a person with access needs, you're not alone, and many other people have the same needs as you when you visit national parks in the United States. What is important is that you feel a sense of enjoyment and wonder and get something positive from your visit whatever your age or stage of learning. This book is written to give you information to plan for your visit and tell you ways of managing your access needs in the park. In its pages, I'll also include a range of techniques and technologies to make visiting easier when you're in your national park and need to know what's available to you as you drive, ride, walk, wheel, or feel your way around.

For professionals who are thinking of making their cultural places more accessible, this book is also designed to provide an overview and support techniques to help you begin the process. Again, these aren't exhaustive lists of techniques, as they're only designed to be starting points for your own professional journey, but they are among the most well-worn paths for developing access. The National Parks Service (NPS) has a long and distinguished history of providing support, education, and services for people with access needs, meaning that you can use their ways of working in your own practice from their examples.

Developing Access or Planning
Your Own Access

Planning accessibility in the great outdoors and isolated visitor centers or campsites in parklands can present a number of difficulties, whether you're a person trying to get access or providing access. The first difficulty is the need to challenge the belief that the ability to learn about or enjoy being in the outdoors, backwoods, backcountry, or the wilderness is based on the ability to be fully mobile, see or hear it, or read, talk, or write about it. The ability to gain something out of cultural places is purely an issue of the mind and the emotions. As I've written before, it's the same way that falling in love is not about the ability to read or write efficiently, because if it were, many of us wouldn't be here.

In my experience of traveling with or supporting people with access issues, changing the belief that all people can't get something out of the natural environment they're a part of is perhaps the biggest barrier to taking trips. But, of course, it should be emphasized that it is very rarely the fault of professionals who work in parks or similar outdoor spaces that this attitude exists. It is also certainly not the fault of people who believe they can't enjoy the environment. I've always found that changing beliefs for everyone is a matter of coming to terms with your hearing and sight loss or your difficulties in learning as something that's a part of you rather than something you constantly have to fight.

The second difficulty is that people with access needs are usually assumed to be like people who have lost their entire ability to see or hear or who have no ability to remember, read, or speak. For instance, when I first started working in classes for people with sight loss, I found that the students were often only offered Braille labels or a few objects they could touch when they sat in class. What's more, when these students were offered a verbal description of the scenery around them or even the room they sat in, the sighted person describing for them rarely spoke about color or shade or was scared of saying phrases like, "I see"—in fact, it almost became a fashion to take out any references to anything "seeable" from sentences altogether. However, this denial of people who had never seen the chance to learn about sight or the denial of people who had seen their own memories was part of a belief that people with sight loss would be offended by vision or they wouldn't understand what was being said.

Shamefully, professionals who developed access in the old days were also taught by academics like me that people with sight problems couldn't understand the visual world intellectually as well as people with full sight. So, alongside the need to challenge notions of access that existed at the time, there was a need to challenge the general assumption that all of our intellectual capacity was based on the ability to see, hear, read, write, and remember.

Thankfully, I also started working in an era when a growing body of the new research by pioneers such as my friend Professor John Kennedy from the University of Toronto was starting to show this assumption was wrong. Thankfully, what we now know is that people with even some remaining sight will understand this vision as much as they do their other senses. What we also know is that people who are born without sight or who only have a memory of sight can understand visual things such as color, foreground, and background.[1]

Generally speaking, access comes in two forms. The first form of access is based on the severity of access need, and this gives rise to what can be called holistic needs, substantial needs, and partial needs.

- Holistic needs are the requisites that affect a whole visit, such as not being able to see or hear at all, not being able to write or speak in what is seen as a regular way at all at the time of visiting a park or a building, or not being able to leave your bed. This kind of access need can mean people will often want a completely different way of communicating or being taught about their

environment, such as through reading Braille, communicating in sign language, or having a virtual tour. Holistic
needs may also mean needing to communicate through
machines or pictures rather than speaking or reading
from lined paper. To put it another way, people with
these needs will need a wholly different way of understanding, sensing, and communicating with the world
around them, although what is communicated or sensed
is still the world we all know in our own way.

- Substantial needs include the requisite to be able to see
  but not make out another person's face, or to be able
  to hear but not make out words from whole conversations, or to be able to move but needing a wheelchair.
  These access needs can make getting to and around big
  outdoor parks or buildings difficult, and yet people with
  these kinds of access needs can communicate ideas and
  have ideas communicated to them using adjusted regular methods. For instance, national park visitors with
  substantial needs may be able to see a mountain in the
  distance using a zoom camera, or they may be able to
  hear the sounds of animals and the rushing wind around
  them but not make out individual birdcalls. In the same
  way, people with these substantial needs may be able to
  communicate in sentences but may only read or write
  them through large-print text.

- Partial needs include the requisite to be able to recognize
  a person's face but not being able to see details, or hearing speech but missing the odd word, or being able to get
  around but needing a cane. These access needs can also
  include finding it difficult to write and read through regular text in brochures or to concentrate for long periods
  on long passages of writing from a guide. For instance,
  people with partial needs may be able to communicate

their ideas verbally but find reading and writing those same ideas difficult; this is because the ability to communicate an idea is not the same as the quality of the idea. Similarly, park visitors with partial needs may find it easy to get to cultural places and be able to use many of the mainstream facilities but find it difficult to access a video without captions or follow a ranger-led program without being able to see their face to lip-read.

The second form of access is based on the age at which people first need support or the age at which they lose their hearing or sight or find it difficult to learn or be mobile. This type of access is often easily overlooked but can be as important as the severity of need because it makes a difference to a person's education, their lifelong experiences of their environment, and even their confidence. If this access is related to the senses, it may also convey an understanding of what hearing or seeing has been. This type of access can also be called born-with needs, assimilated needs, and later-life needs:

- Born-with needs are needs of visitors who lose their sight or hearing or find it difficult to learn or move before the age of three or four (although there is no hard-and-fast rule here, as people often develop at different ages when they're very young). My own studies of access to education show that the key here is that people with access needs have gone through their earliest years, grown up in a family, and learned technologies to support their needs. For instance, because of the nature of some learning difficulties, people are more likely to be born with a particular type of need, such as people who have always found it difficult to read because of dyslexia. These visitors spend their entire life relying more on spoken descriptions, multimedia, or video descriptions or podcasts. Likewise, park visitors without sight in the first four years of life will often have been taught Braille and may have found themselves taught with fewer visual references at school. Consequently, these visitors will most likely appreciate Braille guides. Similarly, they may find it difficult to follow visual information, not because they can't understand it but because they've been taught that they can't understand it or have little use for it. In addition, visitors following ranger-led tours who are born with little or no hearing will be more likely to have learned sign language at school. As a consequence, on their tours, these visitors may appreciate an ASL signer or interpreter—or another form of sign language if needed.

- Assimilated needs are the needs of visitors who lose their sight or hearing or find it difficult to learn or move when they are young but have strong memories of having sight or hearing or being able to learn or move. Generally speaking, visitors with these needs acquired them in their mid- to late childhood or even in adolescence or early adulthood, often between the ages of four and eighteen (although, again, I can't emphasize enough that there are no hard-and-fast rules to picking up these forms of need). Consequently, visitors with assimilated needs may choose to go to and stay in parks in separate groups or with friends and family they feel comfortable around. What's more, visitors with assimilated needs are more likely to want a combination of ways of getting around and understanding their environment or learning about mountains or animals. For example, visitors with hearing problems in late childhood know what it's like to talk even if they do not hear their own or others' voices. However, these visitors will probably have learned sign language, even if they went to regular schools as children or mixed with children who heard. Similarly, visitors with sight loss in late childhood will understand the visual world around them from having had direct experiences of sight but will feel comfortable using Braille and most probably different technologies that convert speech to text.

- Later-life needs are customarily those that are least considered by people developing access for many historical reasons, and yet these are the majority of people with access needs. Also, speaking customarily, visitors who develop later-life needs often develop these needs through the aging process or through illnesses or accidents that can change their lives. This group of people are also less likely to consider themselves as needing help when they visit parks, and why would they? They've gotten through life pretty well up to that point. Alternatively, people with later-life needs may be afraid to ask for help because of their upbringing, or they may not know that there are access facilities out there for them. As a consequence, visitors with later-life needs are perhaps the hardest group of visitors to get to or the hardest group of visitors to persuade that they can still go to national parks, learn about the environment, or see animals in the wild. For example, in my research, I've discovered older people with later-life needs often shun access services after losing sight or hearing and rely on their families or friends who can see or hear better for support. This means that they don't have to stand out from everyone else when they go somewhere. Similarly, people who have learning difficulties later in life, such as visitors with dementia, will also still want to go to parks and outdoor spaces with others they've known most or all of their lives. Similarly, these visitors will want to remember places, things, landmarks, plants, and animals they saw many years ago to help them feel comforted.

The third difficulty people face is the individual upbringing of visitors, whether they have an access need or not, as this means these visitors will all have very different social access needs. In addition, all these different needs will most likely rely more on the early education of visitors, their family background, and the people they've mixed with all their lives rather than their vision or hearing loss or their learning difficulties. In the early millennium, access for people with access needs was about providing everyone with the same experience. Nowadays, however, access is smart, and we deliver bespoke experiences for visitors based on their individual needs rather than their perceived disabilities or their age. In this and other books I've written on this topic, this is referred to as a *visitor-led experience*. What's more, when designing individual access, we can include people with access needs in regular classes, talks, and education programs with visitors who have no access needs if they request it. This means that access to all sites and places outside and inside is now an issue for all park visitors.

Before beginning a vacation or day trip, decide what kind of service you want, make contact with a cultural place, and make clear the type of access service needs you require. Likewise, if access for others in a cultural place or event is planned, the national park or other managed outdoor environment has to be prepared to listen to the individual access needs of its visitors or audiences. For this task, I've developed a simple five-step plan that any professional or volunteer can use to plan their accessible services and people with access needs can use to plan their own visits.

The Five-Step Plan

In my work, I've found that a number of public places and spaces that visitors enjoy have two or three strategies for providing access, and these strategies provide good support for visitors who need it. These strategies are great, developed by dedicated professionals and volunteers, and support people who are, more often than not, what can be called lower on the spectrum of access needs. These strategies are subsequently really important as a means of making for an enjoyable and educationally productive visit; however, as with everything in a nonideal world, there's still lots more to do. For instance, a park or an outdoor attraction's visitor center may have a ramp outside, automatically opening doors out front, and ways of traveling to different floors via elevators; it may have captions on its videos and Braille labels and guides for information; it may even have a website with accessible information that plugs into screen readers and may have alt text on pictures. This doesn't make these cultural places fully accessible, though, as they only consider practical *physical* issues.

In all the best and most accessible places I've ever been to, access strategies consider more than two or three strategies and apply what I've found to be at least five strategies, or what I'm going to call steps, to help people get *richer* experiences, no matter what their needs are, no matter what their level of access needs, and no matter when they first needed help. These five steps are: (1) the ability to go to places with people we know or meet **people we feel comfortable with** through these cultural places; (2) the chance to **learn** while we are in our cultural places; (3) access to **information and information technologies** that will help us get to, get around, learn from, or just enjoy a cultural place; (4) the ability to be in as many of the public **places and spaces** as possible in a cultural place, either in person or through the web; and (5) the ease of access to **mobility** to search for information, to travel, to learn, to go around with someone we know, or to be able to travel around all the public spaces that are available.

For instance, even with a few access needs, I find that I can walk around backcountry and other open spaces with my wife and children comfortably and get a great deal from them. When I get out in the wild, I'm also able to enjoy the wildlife, plants, and trees and maybe go on a guided tour as long as I have sight of whoever's speaking at the time, since I have hearing issues. I can also travel to parks and wilderness in faraway places, and when I visit my wife's family in Italy, I like climbing the local mountains with my son, who is also old enough to enjoy them. I also find it easy to get to the bathroom and eating places in visitor centers or the local towns. This means I can access the public spaces of most rugged and far-flung spaces and places, and I have the physical, sensory, and cognitive mobility to find information online and enough mobility to learn in different spaces around me. I'm also mobile enough to learn and enjoy myself, and most of my friends are mobile enough to join me when I travel to other places, giving me great company.

People higher up the spectrum of access needs, such as my older relatives and friends and the visitors I supported through my work, often need big adjustments to their travel plans, even locally, according to the five steps I outlined. For instance, when we did a coastal walk with my mom a year or two ago, we had to plan ahead carefully and find a route that wasn't too hard for her to walk. We took a tourist train to get there and made sure the seating was easy for her to get into and the stations were easy to get around. For information and learning, we took advantage of local brochures to find out about the area, and I looked up information on the town we visited on the web the night before we traveled. I even made sure I had information on my cell phone and iPad that we could enjoy while we were walking. When we got to our destination, we made sure the paths were sort of flat and not too difficult for Mom. This was imperfect though. For instance, when I walked along a more challenging stretch of beach with my wife and highly energized son and daughter, we had to find a place for Mom to rest, and she couldn't enjoy being with her grandchildren as much as she wanted. This is the reality of even the most well-planned visits.

Given the restrictions that I realize will exist for even the most determined visitor, I have chosen and researched what I feel are a diverse choice of parks that I hope you can truly appreciate on your visits to the great outdoors.

How the National Parks Were Chosen

The choice of national parks in this book is based on a survey of accessibility across the National Parks Service and the access services provided in the individual parks themselves. The process for choosing the parks was rigorous, and as I did with my previous book on cities, I did my best to balance places with different environments, wildlife, plants and trees, historical interest, spectacular views, differing climates, whether they were inland or coastal, whether you could get around the large part of them easily—this being said, they are also naturally difficult to visit out of season in a number of cases, something that is outside the individual park's control, of course.

Importantly, the national parks in this book figure highly on the five steps of the plan for as many needs as possible. For instance, while looking at all these cultural places, I've found many focus on meeting spots for people with higher-on-the-spectrum autism or for people with dementia. What's more, I've found that most places, when providing information, think mostly of Braille, audio description, and captioning for people with vision or hearing loss. This is largely to be expected and plays to people's most essential access needs. From this initial filtering of parks to find a range of visits, I made a final decision about the ten parks according to three choices:

1. The popularity of the parks—that is to say, they are some of the most-visited parks in the United States and among some of the most iconic sites that are recognizable by people outside as well as inside the country. I've also tried to choose parks with interesting activities, education programs, visitor centers, camping or nearby safe and accessible places to stay, as well as good nonaccessible services.

2. The distribution across the United States, representing the north, south, east, west, and of course the middle

of the country. It has to be said at this juncture that the center and western US are represented particularly well, as they have a high concentration of some of the most spectacular national parks. I also thought long and hard about including more distant parts of the country and its incorporated states, such as Hawaii or Puerto Rico. However, I took care to choose parks that represent places that were largely affordable to get to from the mainland if you live in the western or eastern US and places it is possible to drive or ride a train to. This brings me to my third decision.

3. National parks that were relatively accessible by public transportation or car and had largely accessible transport and road networks once you get to them. This didn't have to mean that their transport network is perfect—these are wilderness zones after all—or that they have railways or bus stations on their doorsteps. However, as with my previous book, I decided it was important for visitors to have the ability to get accessible transportation and to be dropped off and from there take relatively simple local transport to the parks if necessary.

Lastly, it should be noted that this book does not have reviews for each national park. This is important, as this book does not try to emulate websites such as Tripadvisor or the other commercial travel guides that give opinion pieces based on the access needs or the preferences or tastes of visitors or customers. In the following choice of national parks, I only give information about the services that are available as advertised at the time of writing. The preference for each one is purely at your discretion and designed as a starting point for your own preparation for visiting these places. It is also strongly advised that you contact the places yourself to arrange your visit if you wish to get the most out of it.

Study Notes

One extra and important issue that I need to include in this preface is how I gathered the information for the different sections in the book through two different types of surveys: survey 1 was of written, video, and audio information on national parks, US states, and accessibility in general; survey 2 was of national parks' access staff themselves. There are two reasons for this: first, as I conducted the information gathering for this study directly via the National Parks Service, I wanted to bring them into the process and ratify as much of the information that I could; second, it is important for professional researchers reading this book as a scholarly resource to appraise my approach for themselves—this is something that is really important in academic communities, even if it is not an academic piece.

The two surveys I conducted were based on three observations from recent academic studies that a number of academics and I had conducted over recent years on this topic:

1. There is a growing number of people in the US who are old and infirm and a growing number of people who are disabled visiting national parks. There is also a growing number of national parks offering facilities, special tours, performances, and courses for people who are elderly or those with disabilities. These facilities, tours, and courses are usually advertised on special web pages or offered directly to people on a visitor database via direct mailings. So more and more people with access needs are being encouraged to visit national parks.

2. Similarly, over recent years, there has been a growth in tourist products available for people who are elderly or those with disabilities, with a growth in travel agencies catering to people with disabilities and developing accessible vacation packages. However, as with all commercial products, these packages largely provide travel

support and accommodation during visits to rural parks but rarely cover the practical or cultural aspects of visits. In addition, despite this growth in both supply of and demand for cultural visits by people who are elderly or those with disabilities, there is a dearth of balanced and independent information on access facilities in national parks as a whole. More importantly, there are few studies that examine best practices and advise and inform on accessible tours, performances, and facilities in national parks. There are also few books on strategies of providing access or accessible technologies that can help visitors make the most of national parks.

Survey 1 of individual national parks was carried out through information available at the parks, brochures, and also books, chapters, papers, and database information on wildlife, geography, and geology in the area of the national parks and their states. Importantly, given the pandemic continuing for much of the development of this book, digital information and tips by colleagues and friends with different access needs were important for providing a direction of study. As the pandemic hit harder and harder during my writing routine, many changes had to be made to my survey, and as travel by colleagues and me was hamstrung, I relied more and more on digital information.

Unusually for me, as an academic researcher and practitioner of twenty-seven years' standing, perhaps for the first time since my beginnings, my survey was exploratory and had no hypothesis. As a consequence, the study's objectives were simply to fill a gap in the knowledge on access in a diverse sample of national parks in the US. Earlier studies had mostly focused on popular urban areas and national monuments with access services; by contrast this survey planned to cover ten exemplar large rural areas alone.

Survey 2 involved an e-mailed questionnaire to those officers with responsibility for access at nine of the ten national parks represented in the chapters; I had covered Yellowstone National Park in an earlier study, so did not repeat the survey with them. When I sent the surveys, I asked each park to return their completed answers within a month. This questionnaire was purposely not too extensive, as the officers were extremely busy, and so I covered only the seven open-styled questions below. The officers were asked to reply via e-mail or, if they preferred, by recording an MP3 voice recording that I would have transcribed if necessary, although none of them chose this method. The seven questions were:

1. How long has your park provided access services for people with disabilities or older people? If you know, please briefly describe how these services began.

2. Could you please provide an overview of the access services you provide for people walking in "off the street," such as information that is available, any technology you provide, or help with mobility? Please feel free to copy and paste if you have prewritten sources or provide a URL if this is publicly available.

3. Do you run classes or specialist tours for people with disabilities or for older people? If you do, could you please provide an example? Again, please feel free to copy and paste existing materials if you have them.

4. Do you have volunteers or employees or subcontract support staff who are trained to work with people with disabilities, such as ASL signers or access coordinators? If you do, please briefly describe what these volunteers or staff do.

5. What activity in your national park or part of your national park would you particularly recommend to an older person or a person with a disability?

6. Can you please describe any particularly successful initiatives that your national park has been involved in? If you have anecdotes or feedback without naming people, please provide these.

7. Do you have an accessible app for your national park beyond the app that is nationally available? If you do, please briefly describe what it does.

In accordance with the research policy at the NPS, after sending my initial surveys to the parks, I was asked to complete an application for a research permit for each park. As part of this permit application, I had to provide a proposal, and many of the parks also asked me to provide peer reviews and proof that the project had been ethically approved. This application was taken forward to the research committee or equivalent in the parks and in most cases was approved within a month, although other parks took up to sixty days to approve it.

As part of the permit application process that the NPS asked me to complete, I had to explain this was an unfunded project and that the results of the survey were to be presented at international education conferences, possibly in journal or blog articles, and in this travel guide; I had to assure the NPS that the survey collected no specimens and did not harm the environment; and I had to detail the nature of the survey answers, how they were to be stored, and that the survey answers would be destroyed after this whole project was finished.

What now follows in the rest of this book is the result of this endeavor.

INTRODUCTION

I wrote this book for all those folks who have access needs, who love to wander, and who don't want to let age, infirmity, or physical or learning issues get in their way. If this is you, in this book, I hope to honor your adventurous nature and try to make your life a little easier as you wander, climb, hike, drive, swim, float, or even hover around a spectacular area of land or water. In this book, I give you information on access, where you can go and make memories, see spectacular mountains and canyons, experience majestic glaciers and rugged coastlines, travel to the shores of lakes so vast you'll not be able to see their furthest shores, and experience rolling tundra, fragrant woodland, or rustic backcountry. It is also designed for those who work with and care for people who have access needs, whether they are family, friends, social workers, or volunteers, to name but a few.

As this book is about access to national parks in the United States, I've also written this book with those who provide access to all forms of outdoor open spaces or a variety of types of visitor centers in mind. In addition, I have written parts of this book for scholars of access, particularly those professionals who design and use accessible technologies, buildings and recreation spaces, and educational programs and tours. For these readers, I've provided extra notes and references to further reading, although you should also note that this is still a generalist guidebook and not an academic resource.

As to why I wrote this book, the idea for the series came out of three observations from my recent work in the field.

First, there is a growing number of people of all ages in the US who have access needs and who want to visit places such as national parks. These visitors may like getting to parks because they rarely get a chance and a reason to travel, or because the parks give them a sense of well-being, even for a short amount of time.

Second, there is also a growing number of national parks that offer facilities, special tours and performances, and courses for people with access needs of all ages. These facilities, tours, and courses are usually advertised on specialist blogs or commercial web pages or parks' websites, or they are offered directly to people through visitor databases at national parks. This suggests that access to tourism, like access to work or access to schools and other forms of learning, is growing in importance and can't be ignored.

Third, there is a growth in specialist tourism providers for people who have access needs, with travel agencies catering to people who need more support, specialized rooms, and so forth and companies developing accessible vacation packages. These packages largely provide travel support and accommodation during visits to hard-to-get-to places and rural parks, meaning that the opportunities to travel to national parks are growing and becoming more achievable.

However, despite a burgeoning growth in the supply of chances to get to and around national parks and the opportunity to make the most of them once you get there, there are few books or other resources on access in a range of national parks. There is also little information about what access means in these parks and how it came about and no single source of information to help you choose what type of park to visit. More importantly, there are no books providing tips, advice, and information on accessible tours, performances, and facilities in national parks. There are also no books on strategies and technologies that can help visitors access a number of national parks and how these came about.

Through this book, I begin readdressing this issue and fill a gap in the sources of information available to you, by developing a book on major national parks in the US that will be updated in the future to keep up with your ambitions. In this introduction, I start this process in two sections: in the first part, I talk about three key terms that I write about throughout this book; in the second part, I present a rundown of the chapters that follow.

Key Terms in This Book

The phrase you'll read most in this book is **access needs**, and you'll have seen it already. Traditionally, access needs are thought of as applying to people who have disabilities or older people who are infirm or who have lost at least part of their memory, vision, or hearing. However, I've found that many of those who visit places like national parks do not wish to be identified by terms that go with their issues, such as deaf, blind, or disabled. Instead, these visitors just want to find practical solutions for the access needs they have and to be with their families. I've also found quite often that many people have preferences for certain types of access, even if they do not identify themselves as having one or more access needs. Examples of these preferences can be the need for larger text, higher-resolution sounds, or more easily read texts, and you don't need to think of yourself as having vision loss or hearing loss to find life more comfortable with these things.

In my work, I have recognized eight experiences as signs of having access needs or an access issue. You don't need to have had all these experiences, but having at least several of these experiences often means you need some form of support. This also does not mean to say that these experiences are fair or morally justifiable; it has more to do with the way that we seem to understand people as needing support.

First, you have an access need if you lack comfort or you experience difficulty when doing regular tasks. This can include finding it difficult or uncomfortable to do regular tasks unaided because of your body or your ability to read, hear, or communicate information to people around you. Regular tasks are things we can be expected to do on an almost day-to-day basis, such as going to a grocery store, and what we find difficult could be something like not being able to hear the person behind the desk, finding it difficult to get into and around the store, or difficulties in reading how much items cost. Regular tasks can also include driving an uncustomized automobile or watching television without additional or alternative information provided through a special button on your remote.

Second is your identity as a person with an access need. Nowadays there is a great deal of emphasis on the need to self-identify or see yourself as similar to others with similar traits. This is a difficult requisite, as people with the same access issues often have different opinions about their disability because of their upbringing or personal point of view. What's more, it can be psychologically difficult for a person to admit to himself or herself that they have vision loss suddenly or to come to terms with the loss of a limb or movement after an accident.

Third is your ability to do regular tasks in comparison to those around you. This is perhaps the hardest issue to accept, as many people who are disabled are also highly intelligent and often highly successful, determined, and capable people in many ways. This also means understanding your ability to act in comparison to people who are not disabled in certain tasks, such as when your speed or dexterity is hindered even with assistance. For instance, you may be a highly successful teacher or businessperson, but after a stroke, you may find it difficult to use a pen on paper without assistance and so have to use accessible technologies you previously hadn't considered normal.

Fourth, your appearance to others around you isn't considered to be that of a regular person. For some people, being able to look, sound, and smell like the norms that are expected in the society that they live in can be difficult, and even if they have an invisible disability, they may find appearing normal is difficult. For example, even if someone is able to speak to other people and be engaging and articulate, they may find it difficult to look at the person they're talking to directly in what can be considered an acceptable way.

Fifth, your reliance and permanent use of what is traditionally seen as an accessible or assistive technology identifies you with other people with access needs that use the same technology. For instance, a person with vision loss often walks with a white cane to identify him- or herself as having access issues; a person with a hearing aid—at least an obtrusive and visible hearing aid—is often seen as having similar issues; and a person with mobility access needs may use a wheelchair, identifying himself or herself to others for this need.

Sixth is the rarity of a person's access issue compared with other access issues of a similar strength. For instance, I am wearing a pair of reading glasses as I write this book, but I am not considered disabled for doing so, even though taking these glasses off while writing would really hinder my job. This is mainly because a large percentage of the world wears some form of glasses.

However, I am thought of as having a disability because I wear a hearing aid, which would provide a similar difficulty as my glasses if removed, largely because having a hearing aid is still seen as pretty rare. Tellingly, significantly older adults are not considered to be disabled simply because of their age, even though many over eighty can't do many things they used to be able to do.

Seventh is the permanence of your access issue and your inability to change your situation, even if you have access to surgery or treatments to lessen it at a particular point in time. For instance, this permanence may be the difference between having a broken leg, which gets better after surgery or being set in a plaster cast, and having a genetic condition that leaves you with permanently weakened limbs. Although both issues may mean you have to use a wheelchair, when the plaster cast is removed you can learn to walk again, whereas the person with the genetic condition will most likely use their chair for life.

Eighth is the strength of a person's access issue in comparison to people with milder issues. There is often a borderline, sometimes one so strong that it has been written into law, that identifies when a person steps over the border into having an access issue that is strong enough to be called disabling.

For instance, sight loss is measured by visual acuity, and so simply having a pair of glasses isn't considered to be disabling, but having a certain weakness of visual acuity is. Similarly, having a slight hearing loss is often not regarded as disabling, and many of us have such a loss. However, having a hearing loss that is so strong it needs to be supported by a hearing aid or having what is called profound hearing loss, where you cannot make out conversations and often have to use sign language to communicate, is thought of as a disability.

Another term you'll come across in the first two chapters is **universal design**. This form of design is used in a variety of different ways, depending on whether you are designing a technology, a vehicle, or something you can't touch, smell, or taste, like an education program. However, the basic principle of universal design is that the design should include as many people as possible—some say this is all people, hence the term "universal," although others would argue this is impossible.

What good universal designers do, however, is plan the design of a technology or course for the most extreme type of use by the minority of the population. This principle is based on the belief that many technologies are designed for the image of an average person, and so if a technology is to be truly inclusive, we should consider the most extremely unaverage person first and move in toward the average person. As Microsoft founder Bill Gates states, "Our vision is to create innovative technology that is accessible to everyone and that adapts to each person's needs."

This leads us to the technologies that support people with access needs and are designed using universal design. Inclusive technologies are "mainstream [technologies] that can be used with either no or minimal adaption by a person with [access needs] as an accessible technology. It is also seen as technology that provides social inclusion, such as communication and interaction, for people with disabilities."[1] Examples of these technologies include modern tablets and cell phones, and they develop inclusion through the physical aspects of design. These inclusive features of design include the look of the interface, the sounds the machine makes and the voice function that it has, the tactile nature of the machine, its size and weight, and the different choices of getting and using the information it produces.

For a number of well-known technology companies nowadays, such as Apple, Google, and Microsoft, the process of building inclusive features into mainstream devices is rapidly becoming a habit. More particularly, the adaptation of lightweight mobile machines means that digital technologies are starting to level the playing field for people traveling around or studying. It also means that formal places and spaces for using technologies, such as offices or classrooms, become less important, and inclusive technologies can relocate to a number of different places, such as buses, automobiles, and hotel rooms, and be used twenty-four hours a day.

Modern inclusive technologies also change the relationship people have with technology, as they change from being machines that we use at work and share with others to emotionally special machines. These machines become our personal possessions like our cars and houses, machines we grow attached to—did our mothers and fathers love the old telephones on the wall and sentimentally talk about them as old friends of the family?

Inclusive technologies nowadays are more than simple information stores or library catalogs; they also become the step-in supporter that we rely on as we do members of our family or friends. This form of flexible technology has been found to be of particular advantage to those with severe access needs in particular. These users can record their lives where normal perception and communication are difficult and instantly access information on day-to-day activities, from catching buses to watching movies to writing this book, in formats that they more easily understand.

Nowadays, technology users with access needs can also easily locate specialist features, such as sign language or Brailling, via the web, which is now the largest and most comprehensive inclusive technology that has ever existed. For this reason, manufacturers like Apple have designed inclusivity around four categories of access needs. These are the need to communicate and learn, the need to see, the need to hear, and the need to use fine-motor skills such as the delicate movement of fingers that so many of us take for granted.

These functions have now given many people with access needs new places to explore, opened up opportunities for travel and learning, and connected users to like-minded people around the world as networks. In the coming chapters, I will look at these technologies in greater detail and how they are changing the way that visitors are engaging with national parks in the US.

What Follows in the Rest of the Book

The following chapters are split into two sections. The first section has two chapters: the first of these chapters looks at the modern history of access in the National Parks Service (NPS) and current policies and directors' orders for fulfilling access; the second chapter looks at the development of inclusive technology as a means of support for people with access needs and a model of using inclusive technology and support.

The second section has ten chapters, one each for a US national park. I have tried to identify traditional nature-based and non-urban national parks spread out almost equally between the east, west, and center of the US. These chapters are planned to provide you with as many varieties of different areas of the US you can visit as possible. Although, I have to be honest, because of the distribution of the most famous and well-resourced parks in the US, the central states turned out to be largely west of center.

The eastern parks represented in these chapters include Acadia National Park in Maine, the Everglades National Park in Florida, and the Gettysburg National Military Park in Pennsylvania. The central parks represented in these chapters include Grand Canyon National Park in Arizona; Rocky Mountain National Park in Colorado; Yellowstone National Park, which is mostly in Wyoming; and Zion National Park in Utah. The western parks represented in these chapters include Denali National Park in Alaska, Olympic National Park in Washington State, and Yosemite National Park in California. You will have noticed that I have also only chosen national parks on the North American mainland, as I wanted to make sure that it was possible, however difficult, to reach each national park via land.

I start this book by looking at the National Parks Service, its development of policies, and the way it fulfills these policies.

Part I
THE NATIONAL PARKS SERVICE AND ACCESS NEEDS

ACCESSIBILITY IN THE NATIONAL PARKS SERVICE

I n this chapter, I write about access services in the National Parks Service (NPS) from a historical perspective, as a resource for two different communities of readers. The first community is visitors with access needs, and the chapter is written to give these readers pointers about how access was developed throughout the service. It is also written to show visitors with access needs what services and facilities are available to them at a national level and the level of importance given them by the NPS. The second community of readers is officers or volunteers wanting to learn about access so they can develop policies and manage and provide access in their own parklands, be they large or small. This community of readers can also include those who are simply scholars of cultural access and the environment and who plan on making a career out of making places and spaces accessible.

As I wrote in the preface, it should be borne in mind that this chapter is based on an interview with an officer at NPS headquarters I named Alfred and a number of parks officers tasked with access at their parks. All these officers provided useful anecdotes, information, and documentation about access planning and delivery that they considered to be relevant to my understanding of the parks themselves and the planning that went on behind the scenes.

It is also important to understand that this chapter is a professional and general history of the NPS, and it will not include social or management theory or an in-depth analysis of practice as academic books do. After all, this book is for a general readership and not an academic volume. However, it is designed to provide a greater understanding of how access has developed over the past fifty years in the NPS's federal-government-run sites, whose reason for being is to balance preserving the environment with providing education and information. Unfortunately, this is a lightly written-about topic and one that I feel is in need of greater attention. It is nice to give them the limelight.

This chapter is set out in the following three sections. The first section explains the history of access and inclusion in the NPS. The second section looks at where the NPS is in terms of its access service at the time of writing. This provides a historical resource and helps readers with access needs know how their services are provided in the current era. But, as I also explain in this chapter, you should bear in mind that this is an ever-changing service and so when this is published, some things may have changed already. The third section is a summary of this history of the NPS.

Early Approaches to Access in the National Parks Service

From Ad Hoc Access to a Whole Parks Approach

It can be said that the history of access in the NPS can be split into two major eras of planning, design, policy making, and management. The first era was the seven years between 1973, when the passing of the first law promoting equality for people with disabilities was passed, and 1980. During this era, a number of national parks developed different specialist services for people with access needs that could be catered to without too much adjustment to the parks' environments or buildings. "The National Park Service began working on accessibility in its park units in the 1970s. This was spurred by passage of Section 504 of the Rehabilitation Act in 1973, which required Federal agencies to ensure that their programs and facilities were accessible to individuals with disabilities."[1]

In my earlier book, *Cultural Heritage, Ageing, Disability and Identity*,[2] I wrote about this period and what was at the time the ad hoc services at Yosemite National Park and the Statue of Liberty based on the requests and needs of visitors. Yosemite in particular turned out to be a popular destination for a group of American Sign Language (ASL) users from local Californian cities, who wanted tours of their park. After this group approached the officer responsible for translation services, someone who was usually responsible for translating spoken or written language, a contract ASL signer was hired to provide signing for all visitors on request.[3] As a consequence, in this era, access services mostly responded to situations that they had to handle on the spot and had little general theory and few models on which to base these services.

The second major era of access began as the 1970s drew to a close, a new decade dawned, and officers based at NPS headquarters in Washington, DC, began to consider a single approach to access in all parks—and what appears to be the first access model of its type in any major national parks service anywhere. This approach was introduced in 1983, was incorporated into visitor accessibility policies,[4] and developed updated NPS management policies to foster consistent inclusion. There were two main reasons for the introduction of these new policies.

First, a growing number of laws specified government-funded institutions had to make their buildings, land, and services accessible to people with a range of what we now regard as access needs—although there was a different terminology for this provision at the time. In addition, officers at NPS witnessed a rise in these services in its parks and in other institutions, such as schools, colleges, and museums. This new delivery of access was part of a new growing social and cultural movement of inclusion for older people and people with disabilities that began in the late 1960s called the Independent Living Movement.[5]

Second, NPS practice was starting to be influenced by the theory of "universal design," that is, the principle that technologies, services, and education can be adapted to fit the needs of all people rather than what was believed to be the majority of the population. In one form or another, the principle of universal design had been around since World War II and had led to innovations in engineering, such as adjustable seating and steering wheels. In this era, however, it was being applied to more intangible innovations, such as individualized teaching strategies.

Universal design in particular was seen as an efficient strategy both in terms of its efficiency and its cost benefits to individual parks. Consequently, NPS undertook a plan to incorporate accessible facilities into all new buildings, facilities, educational programs, and tours, where it was estimated that doing so produced very little increases in costs to the park but large benefits to visitors.

> When facilities and programs are "universally designed" to serve all people, accessibility is generally enhanced for everyone. This is certainly not the case in non-accessible design. In addition, research has shown that, if accessibility is provided at the design stage, the extra cost is negligible. Studies show that the additional cost of making a building accessible is on average 0.5 percent more, and rarely more than 1.0 percent of the total cost. This incremental cost is modest, relative to the large percentage of the population that benefits.[6]

In the seventeen years that followed its initial historic decision, NPS officers made progress by regularizing access across their system based on the traditional understanding of impairment and disability that existed at the time. This understanding largely saw disability as a physical condition and largely focused on two important yet different services for visitors to parks with disabilities. These included providing different forms of information, such as sign language and Braille, and adapting land and buildings to assist people with issues of mobility, particularly visitors who used wheelchairs.

A Change to Access for People with Access Needs

As the twentieth century ended, however, NPS felt that their ways of providing inclusion didn't go far enough and that parks needed to go even further in reaching out to underrepresented communities. First of all, the NPS estimated that fifty-four million Americans could be legally defined as having a permanent disability and that only a small percentage of these were engaging with the national parks system, both as visitors and employees. Second of all, NPS felt that if it was important to make provisions for people who were traditionally considered to have permanent physical disabilities, it was also important to include people with similar needs. These groups included people with invisible disabilities, such as ADHD, heart problems, asthma, and dyslexia; a growing community of older adults (for NPS, these were people over sixty-five years of age); people with temporary disabilities; parents with strollers and devices with wheels, including mobility buggies; and, crucially, the supporters of people with disabilities, including relatives and friends as well as those who were professional supporters. By providing access for these wider communities, NPS believed that the majority of people in the US would benefit directly or indirectly.

In the offices of the NPS, there was also a growing realization that the service had made great strides yet lacked an overall, coherent management strategy for consistently implementing its original aims throughout the country. Subsequently, at the beginning of the new millennium, the director of the National Parks Service developed two sets of what are termed Director's Orders,[7] which were two sets of documents that laid out instructions that had to be followed by all the parks in the NPS. The first set of these orders provided instructions for providing access for visitors, while the second set provided instructions for developing inclusion for NPS staff and those contracted by the service who had access needs.[8]

The main reason for developing these Director's Orders, the NPS stated, was to establish what it called the highest level of reasonable accessibility, not simply to comply with the existing laws on accessibility. In addition, managers who were tasked with access at the time were encouraged to exceed normal standards of access found elsewhere in US society and encourage innovation to develop new forms of access. Both sets of Director's Orders also had five primary objectives: (1) to incorporate the long-range goal of providing high standards of accessibility; (2) to instruct parks on how to implement NPS policies, organizational relationships, and what it termed its implementation strategies; (3) to provide guidance and direction on laws and policies; (4) to instruct parks on the NPS framework to achieve high levels of access; and (5) to implement its model of "universal design."

The major outcome of these two orders was that the NPS also established a chain of command to implement its instructions and policies at individual park level, regional level, and national level. These orders also set out the legal responsibility of each of these staff members. Now, each level of the NPS had staff members, usually middle or senior managers, who were responsible for making sure access and inclusion existed and for implementing access and inclusion and staff members who could act as a point of contact on access and inclusion for the NPS headquarters in Washington, DC, and beyond.

At park level, the orders mandated that park superintendents were responsible for access to concession stands and operators, for other outside companies and organizations, and for volunteers in the park. Those employees designated as park or site accessibility coordinators were also made responsible for access and inclusion for visitors and members of staff. Similarly, at a regional level, regional directors were responsible for making sure that the Director's Orders were being implemented and that laws, regulations, and standards were being upheld throughout their region. In addition, regional accessibility coordinators oversaw the practical development of access for people with access needs throughout their region, including the training of accessibility coordinators and other staff members; the checking of buildings and outside spaces such as paths and trails, amphitheaters, and dockings; and the development of activities offered by parks.

At a national level, a coordinating committee that was formed in the late 1990s, before the Director's Orders, apportioned responsibility for developing and implementing access throughout the NPS, in buildings and on site, and through the design and practice of activities. The committee also fed into access work at a regional level. At its foundation, the committee comprised three associate directors of NPS responsible for park services and education, professional services, and administration alongside representatives of their subdivisions and the equal opportunity program of NPS, many of which had existed for decades.[9]

What was more, the Director's Orders set out the federal laws, regulations, and standards that each park had to comply with to provide access to government-controlled buildings. They also outlined antidiscrimination legislation that they stated was an important aspect of work in this government agency.[10] Importantly, these orders also meant that new levels of accessibility at individual parks, the identification of access barriers, ways of developing policies and guidelines, methods and techniques of improving access, and even the provision of support and training for access staff set a new standard for further models of good practice nationwide in the years that followed.

Putting the Director's Orders in Place

At the time of writing this chapter, this most recent phase in NPS access history had been in place less than a decade. Around 2012, a task force comprised of senior NPS staff and specialists from the regions were appointed to develop a new five-year strategic plan, set out in Director's Order 42. This plan was eventually approved and published in the summer of 2014 as *All In! Accessibility in the National Park Service* and implemented for the first time in 2015.[11]

This five-year plan was said to motivate NPS to prioritize and then expand their access capacity. Subsequently, a group within the NPS called the National Accessibility Board (AXS) was given the simple objective of gathering and analyzing access information, although, as Alfred explained, this information was about access and not the access needs of park visitors: "The National Park Service does not collect any data related to visitors with disabilities."[12] In this period, AXS and the NPS's Office of Public Affairs helped Kiplinger and National Geographic Traveler write articles on accessibility in the national parks system and supported wheelchairtraveling.com in developing the Access to Parks project.

These initiatives were all designed to target resources efficiently, improve existing accessible services, and, as importantly, promote access services to the public at large. At a national level and at local levels, the NPS contacted a number of pressure and advocate groups within the broader disability community to advise on support. For instance, the AXS branch consulted the National Council on Disability and the Consortium for Citizens with Disabilities (a coalition of disability advocacy groups) and the US Access Board to discuss access priorities.

Regionally, NPS also worked with local disability groups, asking them about their experiences of access in individual parks and facilities, and discovered how people with access needs could be more involved in the parks system and this new plan. For instance, Steamtown National Historic Site consulted with people from their own community on NPS training and information and the use of service animals throughout their site. Similarly, staff from the Herbert Hoover National Historic Site were reported to have consulted a number of visitors with sight loss about access to their community, and as a result, someone considered to be an expert on access for people with sight loss was contracted to work on their project.

Technologically, the Harpers Ferry Center for Media Services (HFC) went ahead and developed the Places app, which included an audio description focusing on the landscape, verbalized walking directions, and natural and cultural resources of a number of the most famous sites in the NPS. The app also allowed audio descriptions in a number of pilot visitor centers and exhibits through interactions between their host mobile technologies and iBeacons—electronic devices that could broadcast information to mobile devices in their vicinity[13]—and park audio tour transcripts for those with hearing loss. Early on in the implementation of the five-year plan, the app was piloted at Fort Smith National Historic Site, Klondike Gold Rush National Historical Park, and Herbert Hoover National Historic Site, and after its trial was completed, the app was released free of charge on iTunes in summer 2015.

To implement and oversee its access goals, in 2015 NPS had the equivalent of six full-time access staff and nine regional accessibility coordinators. It was the job of these officers to create accessible information on access for the parks, develop training on a national and at regional levels, and look after those tasked with accessibility in the parks. Furthermore, to provide a specific focus for evaluating its five-year plan, NPS included three overarching goals in its original documentation. These were: (1) create a welcoming environment, increasing the ability to serve visitors and staff with disabilities; (2) ensure that new facilities and programs were inclusive and accessible; and (3) make existing facilities, programs, and services more accessible.

To tackle goal 1 throughout the US, a number of departments in NPS headquarters were given scope to act as leaders and advocates for inclusion and access throughout the system.[14] Beyond the internal development of internal development of access, AXS also met with a number of federal government departments[15] to discuss the employment of people with disabilities at NPS. They also consulted the Corporation for National and Community Service to consult on NPS youth initiatives and met with the national Disability Policy Group to discuss access in all government organizations.

In addition, as part of its strategization of access at regional level, the Coordinating Committee[16] was expanded to include people with responsibility for access in the parks and the regions, in an effort to be less "Washington-centric." This committee met regularly online to provide better coordination between parks and regions, although because of the diverse nature of the parks, differences in the way that access was applied were still said to remain. Furthermore, hundreds of rangers, superintendents, and those who ran private concessions across the system had accessibility training, which was offered online and in person by the National Center on Accessibility (NCA), experts on disability access, and NPS access staff.

To tackle goal 2, NPS worked on models of good practice across NPS regions through research and the continual analysis and documentation of strategies that worked. They also took a look at projects that had caused problems in the past, tried to identify their pitfalls, and provided working practices that sought to avoid such issues in the future. As with other strategies in this new approach, NPS found that staff from the regions who knew and had worked with access strategies for some time were adept in their ways of working already. However, this level of service was often uneven, and there were also parks where highly targeted training was needed, and parks that had less capacity and resources to implement access, or at least their services, needed to be improved significantly.

By 2015, the NPS reported that its centers specializing in accessibility had dealt with hundreds of requests from parks around the US, and almost 250 studies of quality assurance reviews that included accessibility had been carried out. The NPS also worked with a number of disability community groups on universal-designed facilities, technologies, and services. In addition, formal and informal contributions from communities of people with disabilities were used to evaluate projects when they were first developed.[17]

After a year of the new plan, highly innovative technologies to promote "virtual" accessibility using their philosophy of universal design for all was also announced, and this included the use of the Places app. This led to an evaluation of the app, particularly its accessibility for visitors with sight loss, and the results of this evaluation were presented to the public, practitioners, and academics.[18]

To tackle goal 3, NPS's primary task in 2015 was to write a task agreement between them and NCA. Consequently, a number of parks throughout the US reviewed their accessibility offerings with officers from NPS headquarters or regional officers in order to change their buildings, sites, and practices and formed their own internal teams to improve the quality of their services.[19]

A year after, NCA established standard operating procedures for reviewing access in parks, and a number of NPS centers developed the Targeted Accessibility Improvement Program (TAIP), which aimed to improve accessibility in what were felt to be key parks. To implement these new procedures, nine parks were chosen as part of the pilot.[20] This also led to highly specific funding packages for parks with large numbers of visitors who had particularly important access needs, and prioritized funding for those parks that were happy to match-fund this extra resourcing from their own regular budgets.

Current Accessibility in the National Parks Service

Finishing the NPS Five-Year Plan

As I write this chapter, the NPS is in the final year of its five-year plan and developing new access arrangements and strategies. NPS and the rest of the world are also going through what we hope are the final throes of the COVID-19 pandemic that has not just rocked the way we all behave but changed the way we think about our environment and the quality of our lives. This had and continues to have a dramatic effect on how national parks work around the US and also the way that access is delivered. We're also in a period of financial uncertainty where federal budgets will have to be reset, making future planning difficult and possibly putting further progress in jeopardy.

To talk about the implications of the current pandemic would take a whole new book, one that I don't have the information to write at the moment—although it would make a great study for someone someday. So what I am writing in this section represents the information I've managed to gather at the time of writing and also what I hope will be the foundations for the progress that the NPS had in the past and what it plans to continue in the present. Only time will tell.

At the time I first wrote this chapter, the National Parks Service had five officers who were dedicated to accessibility full time throughout the US. Three of these officers, specialists in accessibility throughout the parks system, were based in its Washington, DC, headquarters and provided training and technical assistance to park units. These Washington-based officers were also responsible for setting out what was going to become future access policy at the NPS. In addition, the NPS continued to employ a management structure from its Washington headquarters via its National Accessibility Branch. This branch worked via an equivalent service in its regional offices through to individual parks to ensure responsibility for access facilities and services and standards of accessibility.[21] There was also one park in the system that had a full-time accessibility specialist, and there was an officer who focused on accessible exhibits and media at the national level too.

Given the number of parks in the system, this meant that much of the application of the five-year plan was regional, and much of the responsibility for planning and implementing access lay with individual access officers in individual parks. Many of these park officers were often part-time workers or fit in this role with other roles such as park ranger or superintendent. This said, Alfred explained that "each of the parks in the system and every regional office [of the NPS] was expected to have an accessibility point of contact who focuses on accessibility up to 20 percent of the time."

Perhaps the most important innovation in the five-year plan that had an impact on the way the parks delivered access was the regularizing of visitors with disabilities: recognizing they wanted to visit with nondisabled visitors and trying to address individual's access needs. This strategy also meant that it was important for the

NPS *not* to automatically see people with similar impairments, such as sensory loss or learning needs, as a single community and one in need of separate support, programs, or tours—this was unless individual groups asked for these services directly.

This philosophy also acknowledged that visitors with access issues may have a number of needs, such as issues with mobility, reading, or memory. As a consequence, grouping people into single communities based on the belief that they would only need support for certain types of loss meant that many people didn't have all their needs supported properly and they missed out on many of the parks' experiences. In practice, this meant that parks decided not to design services for people with what were felt to be individual forms of loss or impairment, such as vision or hearing loss. Instead, NPS encouraged individual parks to look at the individual in the round, to assess their individual needs, and to tailor technologies and experiences accordingly.

> It is very rare that park units offer tours specifically for persons with disabilities. Our preference is to modify programs open to the general public to ensure they include individuals with disabilities. However, we would accommodate an advance request from groups of individuals with disabilities who were traveling together. For example, if a large group of individuals who are Deaf wanted a tour with a sign language interpreter, a unit would arrange it.[22]

Equality of Provision across the NPS

In this equation, all parks were not equal, however, as the nature and size of a park could provide natural advantages or disadvantages to those who were providing access for those who needed it. For instance, larger, better-known parks had more rangers, superintendents, and resources and so could provide more specialized forms of access services. These parks also had more concessioners who were willing to invest in the infrastructure of the park, or these parks had overall budgets that had been much larger even before the development of access began. Subsequently, and although they welcomed more visitors, these parks could also afford to contract specialist staff on a regular basis, develop their own knowledge of accessibility in their particular environment, and integrate accessibility into their park's culture.

Elsewhere, other national parks had more recently updated or built new facilities, such as visitor centers or campsites, during the period of the five-year plan or had been at a point where they had to update their facilities. This meant that these facilities were entitled to extra funding to integrate accessibility into the structure of the center or the campsite, particularly if they could match funding that was provided by the NPS headquarters. "[There] are park units that have areas which were designed to be more accessible than others and tours that were offered accordingly. For example, we have a number of caves where only a portion is accessible for wheelchair users, so the unit would arrange for visitors in wheelchairs to experience that portion of the cave."[23]

However, despite their diversity, almost all parks at the time of writing offered a number of core access services to all their visitors, often without any extra charge to the visitor. These services included audio descriptive tours or accessible descriptions that could be downloaded from apps or websites; access to Braille materials, such as brochures or educational materials for the programs run by the park for visitors with vision loss, although in many cases the parks did not have their own facilities and had to contract in Brailling; the ability to provide tactile maps and exhibits to visitors with vision loss, although these differed greatly between parks and, as I wrote above, the larger parks were often more able to develop these alternative formats while smaller parks found it more expensive within their budgets; closed- and open-captioned and audio-described videos, which were often produced by outside agencies for the parks and so again favored the larger, wealthier parks; and captioned and audio-described interactive exhibits or whole displays that were available to people who asked to see them, although a number of parks had these on display constantly. There was also a whole NPS app that was designed to promote accessibility, provide practical information, and act as an e-learning technology, although it was noted by a number of people I communicated with in the parks service that not all parks used it.

In addition, many park buildings almost always had ramps fitted as standard, as well as elevators and disability lifts to different floors or levels within buildings for visitors with issues of mobility. However, this was occasionally restricted in parks with more historical buildings and environments that couldn't be bashed around or changed easily or where there were restrictions placed on their heritage by federal laws or UNESCO. Furthermore, almost all parks at the end of the five-year plan had accessible restrooms, accessible parking, lowered counter spaces at front desks, and other features that Alfred felt should be "common to [public] buildings." All of these parks were also assisted in providing these facilities by the three staff working out of the NPS Washington office, who also helped with developing newer policies and putting plans into action locally.

Finally, to recognize all these endeavors and to reward parks who managed to exceed the expected levels of accessibility standards in the NPS, the National Accessibility Branch also launched a series of annual access awards for parks. To be presented one of these awards meant that the park completed particularly strong, unique projects that were related to progressive accessibility or showed a sustained commitment to accessibility over the course of a particular year.

Summary

The NPS has had increasingly accessible parks since their inception in the early twentieth century, although this was rarely thought of as a social or cultural issue in this early era of the NPS and more as a moral duty. Since the 1970s, and largely because of early federal legislation on building access, it can be said that the NPS has progressed through two highly distinct eras of access. The first era was the provision of ad hoc access and was largely developed on the initiative of individual parks in the system. As so many different parks had distinctive environments, budgets, and levels of protection, this made standardization difficult.

The second era came in the late 1970s and early 1980s through the development of a coherent accessibility policy that was planned on the principles of universal design—that is to say, the design of technologies, environments, and even classes to include as many people as possible. These principles were the foundation of a series of Director's Orders, a set of instructions that were applied to all national parks nationally and came from the very top of the organization.

The latest stage of access and inclusion is coming to an end at the time of writing this book. This stage started with a further set of Director's Orders in 2014, which unveiled a five-year plan that began in 2015 and contained three accessibility goals: (1) a welcoming environment needed to be created; (2) new facilities and programs had to be accessible; (3) existing facilities, programs, and services had to be more accessible.

The most important element of this plan was the support of all people with access needs rather than assuming that people with disabilities should be identified as "disabled people" or identified themselves as "disabled people," unless they specifically said they did. To put it another way: (1) it was recognized that there were people with access needs who wanted to see themselves as being part of an impairment community; (2) however, it was also recognized that many people with disabilities who visited national parks wanted to be regular visitors and not separated or seen as different.

In the next chapter, I look at the development of the notion of universal design in learning and technology, to provide both a context for the support provided by the ten national parks and a learning resource on the philosophy of universal access.

Appendix

In its 2015 Director's Orders, the National Parks Service gives additional sources of information that are external to its service. These are particularly good resources for those officers wanting to plan access in other parks or cultural venues. For this reason, I am adding them below for your use:

- **National Center on Accessibility (NCA)**—https://nca online.org—access information for those planning to visit parks and the like or to attend education programs and recreation areas and programs; training programs and opportunities; technical assistance for park and recreation professionals; and research and demonstration projects.

- **US Architectural and Transportation Barriers Compliance Board (US Access Board)**—www.access-board .gov—Provides information on: current status of accessibility standards and proposed accessibility guidelines; future meetings of the Access Board and minutes to previous meetings; Access Board newsletter and other publications; information on activities of ongoing projects.

- **US Department of Justice ADA Home Page**—www .ada.gov—Provides comprehensive information on the requirements of the Americans with Disabilities Act, updates on new developments, and technical assistance information.

- **US Census Bureau**—www.census.gov/people/disabil ity—Provides information on the Office of Statistics and on disability population statistics.

- **National Institute on Disability and Rehabilitation Research (NIDRR)**—www.acl.gov/about-acl/ about-national-institute-disability-independent-living

-and-rehabilitation-research—Provides information on NIDRR projects, publications, and other disability and rehabilitation resources.

- **Disability and Business Technical Assistance Centers**—https://disabilityinfo.org/fact-sheet-library/legal/ada-disability-and-business-technical-assistance-center/—Provides information on technical assistance for entities covered by Title II and III of the ADA; listings of regional centers; and the most frequently asked questions on the provision of access for people with disabilities.

- **International Disability Access Symbols**—https://graphicartistsguild.org/downloadable-disability-access-symbols/—Provides information on international symbols organized by the Graphic Artists Guild Foundation and symbols for downloading, including audio description, volume control, sign language interpretation, closed captioning, and others.

- **Center for Universal Design**—https://projects.ncsu.edu/ncsu/design/cud/—Provides information on principles of universal design and the concept of designing products and environments to be usable by all people.

- **Trace Research and Development Center**—https://trace.umd.edu/—Provides information on interdisciplinary research, development, and resource materials on technology and disability and recommendations for designing accessible web pages.

- **National Center on Accessible Media (WGBH-Boston)**—ncam.wgbh.org—Provides information on research and development for accessible media; Rear-Window movie captioning system; and recommendations for accessible web pages.

- **Project ACTION**—www.projectaction.org—Provides information on technical assistance programs promoting accessible transportation systems within communities throughout the US.

- **Beneficial Designs**—www.beneficialdesigns.com—Provides information on rehabilitation engineering and design and the innovative Universal Trail Assessment Process for mapping levels of difficulty for trails.

- **Wilderness Inquiry**—www.wildernessinquiry.org—Provides information on outdoor adventures for people of all ages and abilities.

- **TransCen, Inc.**—www.transcen.org—Provides information on accessibility standards, training programs and opportunities, and additional accessibility resources.

ACCESSIBLE TECHNOLOGIES FOR VISITORS WITH ACCESS NEEDS

I n the last chapter, I described how the National Parks Service (NPS) designed their access services using universal design, that is to say, the design of technologies, facilities, buildings, and even education to suit all visitors, not just the majority of visitors.[1] In this chapter, I write about how this idea is used in accessible technology, and I start you thinking about how you can use such technologies to learn, to teach, and to get the most out of your visits or help your visitors if you are tasked with making your site accessible.

In these pages, I'm also going to describe a way of thinking about how technologies you make use of every day can be used more accessibly and inclusively. I then look at ways that educators like me work with these technologies, and show you how the development of modern mobile learning using your cell phones, tablets, or fancy laptops with touch screens and detachable keyboards represents an advance in accessible technologies for all.

As with the last chapter, this chapter is written with two communities of reader in mind. The first community of readers is people who teach or lead tours in the outdoors or readers who provide or are considering providing access for a cultural park. This community can also include teachers or those providing support to people with access needs, including families and friends. The second community of readers is visitors with disabilities or older people. If this is you, I aim to let you know about approaches to integrating universally designed, inclusive technologies in your own support and learning in national parks and to help you choose the best forms of technology for your visits, for searching for and downloading information, or for virtually touring parks online.

The chapter is broken into four sections. The first section examines technologies for learning and supporting people with access needs and the integration of ways of learning and teaching using these technologies. In this section, I also examine how technology has been included in modern education and a way of using digital technologies through substitution, augmentation, modification, and redefinition (SAMR) of learning tasks. The second section describes what technological access needs are, how accessible technology can support people with access needs when they're learning about or in outdoor education, and how these technologies have changed the way we teach and support people with access needs. The third section looks at how we are changing our understanding of accessible technology and presents a case study of mobile learning and accessible learning. The fourth section summarizes the other three.

How Technologies for Support, Learning, and Teaching Developed

The first studies of technology in formal learning started in ancient Greece as early as 500 BCE;[2] however, an understanding of the importance of technology in teaching and learning has only recently been fully realized. It took many years for comprehensive histories to be written on this topic, particularly those relating to electronic media in teaching.[3] This is unfortunate, as we now realize that technology often plays an important role in the delivery of teaching and learning and has been involved in the understanding of learning processes from the earliest psychological experiments on learning.

At its simplest, early in the twentieth century, the earliest behavioral experiments devised to mimic learning, such as those of the famous Russian psychologist Ivan Pavlov, used devices such as bells and metronomes to provide stimuli for behavior.[4] Similarly, Pavlov's American contemporary Edward Thorndike designed a technological innovation, the puzzle box, to mimic a complex form of learning behavior.[5]

In the middle of the twentieth century, Thorndike's contemporary and fellow American Buhurus F. Skinner designed similar cages with levers to deliver punishment and rewards.[6] In his most popular work, *Beyond Freedom and Dignity*, Skinner took this notion of educational technology further still by suggesting that students could do away with traditional lessons and teachers.[7] Instead, Skinner proposed that people should use technology to learn in their own time through devices meant to provide positive and negative stimuli, dependent on whether students learned a given piece of knowledge in a correct or incorrect way. And yet, despite these references to technologies to support the development and application of our understanding of teaching and learning, the *nature* and *role* of technology as a means of learning support has too often been considered to be superfluous to the act of learning in all but high-tech subjects.

Digital educational technologies have, however, started to become established in other learning contexts in more recent years. Around thirty years ago, for instance, educators in distance and correspondence colleges started to realize that not only scientifically measurable behavior but the technological environment of education could be equally important to teaching and learning. Consequentially, interactive learning technologies became of considerable value to new forms of undergrad and postgrad course delivery, particularly for those students who could not afford to make it to school fulltime. This was learning that had previously been delivered through one-way communication, such as television, telephone, and radio, or through paper files, but which could now be delivered through home PCs or laptops.

With the advent of the World Wide Web, the Internet, and social media, the use and power of communication technologies in developing learning via increasingly sophisticated and digitized technologies quickly revolutionized teaching. So nowadays, online courses and Massive Open Online Courses (MOOCs) can be conducted entirely through web-based technologies such as Second Life, the fantasized, virtual world in which human beings are represented through their own avatars and can live life without gravity or geographical boundaries.

What is perhaps most important to identify in this technological revolution is that there are two particular eras that have altered our thinking on technology in mainstream learning since the introduction of electronic technology: the immovable computer era—that is to say, computers that were restricted to physical desktops because they were so large, heavy, and connected to cables—and the mobile computing era—that is to say, small, light computers that are connected to Wi-Fi and that can be carried around easily.[8]

The immovable computer era itself can also be said to have had two separate phases of technological introduction. The first phase was the introduction of the first commercial computers in the 1960s, that is to say, computing technology that did not take up a whole room; although it did not change learning, it allowed learners to use technologies. The second phase came in the 1990s and involved the use of computing technology in nontechnological environments. This phase began with the introduction of teachers' computers, projectors, and interactive computer-driven whiteboards, which were otherwise known as smartboards. In this phase, students started to use computers for nontechnological as well as high-tech subjects. Consequently, with this second era came changes in the way that we learned and a recognition of digital technologies as a way of teaching and supporting learners. This second era subsequently gave rise to new ways of learning and teaching, ways that did not simply identify technologies as they were in previous eras but organized these technologies according to their learning purpose.

One popular and modern way of organizing technologies of learning to ways of learning is the modern acronym SAMR. This system categorizes the application of technology for learning as substitution, augmentation, modification, and redefinition.

Substitution and **augmentation** describe the way that traditional learning activities, such as writing or drawing, have been changed into like-for-like digital activities. For example, decades ago, a small number of learners were taught typing skills in specialist secretarial classes on traditional typewriters. Nowadays, digital technologies have substituted word processors for these older typewriters and augmented typing pads on-screen. In doing so, they have also changed the learning of a relatively specialist skill to a regular skill that almost all learners use in regular classes nowadays—or even in the street. Similarly, the introduction of digital technology has also led to the augmentation of tools that were once mechanical, such as the shredding or filing of documents, to digital equivalents, such as the use of pictures of waste bins or folders on computer desktops.

Modification and **redefinition** describe the way that old-fashioned learning activities have been completely changed into completely new, digital ones. For example, texting has completely taken over from handwriting messages or writing letters and sending them with a stamp. Social media has created new ways of keeping in touch with friends and family—or meeting friends online you haven't even met in real life. Internet search engines, like Google, have also revolutionized the way we look for information, and suddenly the learning skills we once needed in order to use dictionaries or reference books require modified digital skills or skills that have been completely redefined.

You could even say that even technologies that were first designed to substitute for old skills are now modifying the skills that we have to learn. For instance, new word processors have not only substituted for and augmented older functions; they also have brand-new tools that modify our ways of working. New skills we use to word process include the ability to save different versions of files, the ability to e-mail directly from a document, and the ability to change a paper-looking document into a web page. Similarly, tasks we were once taught through the use of old-fashioned technologies such as keyboards have been completely redefined and are now possible through digital inputs such as voice commands or swiping and tapping touch screens. This new digital revolution we are a part of subsequently means that twenty-first-century learners need a whole new set of digital learning skills.

So how has technology changed the life and education of people with disabilities and older adults? What is more, can SAMR be applied to universally designed technologies that support people in cultural sites, such as national parks?

Disability, Learning Difficulties, and Accessible Technology

As I wrote in the introduction, the word "disability" has come to mean many things, although disability was not a widely used term until the last quarter of the twentieth century.[9] The contemporary origins of its meaning date back to eighteenth-century society, when it was believed that certain types of people were incapable of working or learning. This community of *disabled* people was increasingly marginalized, and if they came from working or underclass families, they often had to resort to either begging in city streets, because of urbanization, or to highly menial work, such as selling matches, to scratch out a living.

Although there were able-bodied beggars at the time, people with disabilities were found to be resorting to begging in increasing numbers in this era.[10] In fact, for at least one section of society, people with what are now called disabilities were seen to be particularly successful as beggars or were seen as a class apart and more deserving of charity than those people who, it was felt, could do physical work. However, to a more traditionalist section of society, this belief in the inferiority of people with disabilities also stereotyped this community as lazy and immoral. This belief was compounded, as disabilities were also often linked with diseases, such as syphilis, that were caused by "immorality" or were prevalent among the "lower classes," many of whom were themselves often considered to be mentally subnormal.

In response to what was considered to be this social problem, a number of charitable institutions were first founded in Europe and then North America, parts of Asia, and Australasia to institutionalize people with different forms of disability. These institutions were designed to educate people with disabilities and either provide an intellectual "enlightenment" or teach what was felt to be a meaningful trade that would discourage this community from begging. Although initially developed for adults, these institutions also were later adapted to cater to children and took on a more educational and training role in the process.

Although people with different human issues, such as vision and hearing loss and mental health conditions, were kept in separate institutions from the eighteenth century to around the first half of the twentieth century, there was a tacit understanding that people with disabilities, particularly physical disabilities, were exposed to similar social struggles. This understanding was first recognized in a small way in a number of countries throughout North America and Europe from as early as the latter years of the nineteenth century and the earliest years of the twentieth century. As a consequence, a few countries including the US passed laws to support people with disabilities still living in poverty or attempted to develop more meaningful educational opportunities for these communities. However, despite these early initiatives, prejudice against people with disabilities was still widespread.

As the twentieth century progressed, so did social attitudes toward people with disabilities, particularly after World War I when more adults than ever before returned home from fighting having been scarred for life. These former soldiers, sailors, and fliers weren't seen as incapable but as heroes, and it became an insult to society to cast them aside, given the horror they had been a part of.

This change of attitude inevitably led to the development of new institutions that promoted learning and retraining for people who developed disabilities as adults. It also led to a small but burgeoning movement to make social and cultural institutions more accessible for people with impairments. This was not just inclusion and accessibility as a form of charity or pity, but access and inclusion as a human right for those who were now regarded as equals. In the latter years of the twentieth century, following World War II and smaller conflicts such as the Korean and Vietnamese wars, this recognition of human rights for communities of physically disabled people was extended to others who had access needs. This led to the belief that individuals with combinations of cognitive, developmental, emotional, and communication issues, such as dyslexia, autism, Down syndrome, and dementia, were entitled to similar human rights.

In the latter decades of the twentieth century and as history spilled over into the new millennium, equality and greater opportunities for people with disabilities became a subject of new politics in Westernized countries. This subject also led to a debate on the equality of disabled people, which became a theme for national governments and international institutions such as the World Health Organization (WHO). Consequently, many institutions wrote definitions of disability that increasingly incorporated the social and cultural factors that people with disabilities and older people face and described how we think about disability as much as the bodily or physical issues that they engender. This idea was particularly reflected in the UN's last definition of disability:

> The term persons with disabilities is used to apply to all persons with disabilities including those who have long-term physical, mental, intellectual or sensory impairments which, in interaction with various attitudinal and environmental barriers, hinders their full and effective participation in society on an equal basis with others. . . . Disability resides in the society not in the person.[11]

Technology, Disability, and Support

The technologies developed to support people with disabilities and older people were initially known as medical or assistive technologies and, in the latter years of the twentieth century, were broadly defined as "any item, piece of equipment, or system, whether acquired commercially, modified, or customized, that is commonly used to increase, maintain, or improve functional capabilities of individuals with disabilities."[12] However, as soon as institutions for people with disabilities developed, technologies and adapted teaching methodologies evolved, articles were written, and associations of teachers and innovators were encouraged to innovate new ways of learning and supporting through technology.

For example, special classes and institutions have become expert at producing their own material in languages such as Braille, providing magnifying lenses, and developing new ways to use mobility devices, such as walking canes, white canes, and wheelchairs. With the introduction of mobile electronic audio devices also came the increased use of technologies such as hearing aids and amplifiers for people with hearing loss and radio transmissions for people with vision loss. Later, more mobile digital technologies provided further help in making writing and reading information available. Assistive apps also helped to overcome barriers to learning through, for instance, audio descriptions of books and artworks, enlargement or recoloring of text on-screen, and the representation of sound as text.

In keeping with SAMR, so-called assistive technologies led to learning strategies that incorporated the use of devices to enhance learning and accessible support outside regular teaching institutions, such as special schools and colleges. Substitution slowly allowed mainstream schools to teach students with disabilities about technologies that could help them access regular classes. For example, students who had difficulties reading could record their teachers' voices in class using specialist digital recorders and then play them back through MP3 devices in lieu of note taking.

Similarly, other assistive technologies were developed to enlarge or color text on computer screens to substitute for traditional reading materials. Furthermore, augmented skills were taught through the use of software such as JAWS and other screen readers that synthesized voices for computer users with sight loss or tools that synthesized voices for people with conditions such as motor neuron disease.

As well as those assistive technologies that could *enhance* learning, there were also assistive technologies that could radically *transform* learning and support. For example, in the twentieth century, assistive software and hardware began to redefine how students were taught to read and produce writing through devices such as portable digital Braillers and Braille readers to assist with tactile literacy for people who are blind.[13] Similarly, devices were developed that could modify the way that traditional skills in mainstream schools and colleges were used to support a growing number of learners with disabilities attending these institutions.

However, there is a problem with the theory that assistive technologies can provide full inclusion in all situations and all learning environments. In itself, assistive technology too often separates people with disabilities from those without disabilities and provides a reason not to include people with disabilities in all regular classes, tours, or programs. In many cases, assistive technologies are large and cumbersome, and the skills needed to use them by people who support people with disabilities mean that they are often installed in special spaces in galleries or rooms in museums or visitor centers. This leaves less social inclusion in the lives of people with disabilities.

Furthermore, many people with disabilities and their teachers, supporters, and families have found that many assistive technologies are prohibitively expensive. This is largely because they are designed and manufactured in small numbers, making them more expensive than mainstream, mass-produced technologies. In addition, although the name "assistive technology" is designed to signify the assistance nature of technology, this emphasis on difference and help often means that people with disabilities are separated from nondisabled people so they can be taught the skills necessary to use these technologies, or it means that people with disabilities are still dependent on people without disabilities.[14]

Redefining Assistive Technology as Universally Designed, Inclusive, Accessible Technology

For all these reasons, traditional assistive technologies can provide some of the last cultural and social barriers to accessibility and inclusion for people with disabilities and older people. In the past, this has been a problem of assistive engineering and design, as these disciplines are too often developed and written about by able-bodied people trying to imagine what it is like to have a disability. Moreover, engineers and designers more often than not fall prey to social and academic stereotypes. Subsequently, traditional assistive technologies are physically and socially awkward machines.

There are also socially and culturally negative aspects of traditional assistive technologies that affect the self-esteem of students who have to use them. In particular, I've found that traditional assistive devices often single out people with disabilities in a crowd, and this can stigmatize people with disabilities when they try to be part of mainstream communities.[15] I've also found that learning institutions such as schools, colleges, and national parks themselves also do little to help the *process* of developing methods of including people with disabilities through assistive technology. This is because many educators focus on the mechanical and electronic properties of hardware and software, rather than thinking about the social acceptability of their design or the ability of their usage to blend in, in regular environments.

Moreover, despite the development of new forms of regular learning technologies through innovations such as mobile digital learning, there have been embarrassingly few studies on the compatibility of these new technologies when they're used with assistive devices. This is in spite of the fact that many modern mobile technologies now have assistive functions built in. This creates a problem in providing learning and support for people with disabilities and highlights the need for a reevaluation of technologies as machines that can support all people, not only the nondisabled majority.

This reevaluation always leads me to two more questions in my practice: (1) What is inclusion in technology? (2) How can technologies be more fully inclusive?

In answer to the first of these two questions, contemporary mobile consumer technologies are at last starting to realize that they need to be used with either no or minimal adaptation by people with disabilities. What's more, technologies that provide communication and interaction with others are increasingly making people with disabilities feel less vulnerable and less socially isolated. So, in order for technology and the design of technology for people with disabilities to be more useful, accessibility is slowly entering the mainstream. In addition, modern mainstream manufacturers are designing machines that are closer to the theory of universal design promoted by the National Parks Service that I wrote about in the last chapter. This brings the study of assistive technology in line with other forms of inclusion that have gone before it, which state that all students should have social equality with each other in all environments.

In answer to the second question, it is arguable that the terminology used to describe technologies, learning, and support in regular environments itself needs to be looked at carefully. Possibly the first way this is being done is to rename assistive technology as universally designed, inclusive technology for learning and support.[16] This has helped to shift the focus of design and engineering away from a technological dependency culture of people who are disabled and move it toward the inclusiveness of the technology and the communities they supply, as well as the social and cultural inclusion issues they are beginning to address.

The second part of this process is the redefinition of engineering and design themselves to make them socially fit for people with disabilities. That is to say, engineering is trying to make its practice be about perceived practical measures, making it more customer led and focusing more and more on the social individuals for whom technology is created. This has increasingly been achieved by training and encouraging people with disabilities to create, or at least including people with disabilities in the design process, and not just using the community as end-user testers. In this way, people with disabilities are also being seen as people who have valuable ideas and can contribute to their societies. As this is being achieved, albeit slowly, we can look at SAMR in a way that emphasizes redefinition of tasks as being the least important purpose of universally designed, inclusive technologies, and substitution as being the most important role for these technologies.

For example, cell phone and tablet manufacturers now have a number of universally designed, inclusive features that are fitted as standard, such as voice functions to identify objects for people who have sight loss or other forms of reading issues, text on-screen for people with hearing loss, software and apps for enhanced reading to support people with learning disabilities, zoom camera facilities for users with low vision, and functions for changing color to photo negative. These are functions that previously took a whole assistive technology for each function but are nowadays a simple matter of adjusting the settings when you first buy your technology from your regular store.

Summary

Accessible technologies have helped many people for decades and have largely been thought of as a force for good for people with disabilities and older people. However, engineering has been slower than many other parts of society to evolve and to include all people, no matter what their access needs, in regular spaces and parks. This has largely been because the focus of the engineering and design of assistive learning technologies was largely their technical capacities and their perceived functions, rather than their form or their ability to include people with disabilities in all mainstream social environments.

Unfortunately, such design issues were often the result of a lack of understanding by nondisabled designers and engineers, who often did not grasp the true issues surrounding disability. SAMR and universal design applied to learning and support that use regular technologies illustrates this point well. Consequently, for those who are planning or managing access and inclusion in their own institutions, what is needed is to consult and include users of technologies at every stage of the process of using design for accessibility and not just use people with disabilities and older people as part of a testing process. More importantly, in your own practice, it is important to redefine assistive technology as universally designed, inclusive technology. This is technology that can more easily include people with disabilities and learning difficulties in all aspects of life. Although this process has started with mobile technologies and learning, there is still a long way to go, and this is something you should consider yourself a part of when designing your own access and inclusion.

Part II

TEN NATIONAL PARKS

CHAPTER THREE
ACADIA, MAINE

Address: PO Box 177, Bar Harbor, ME 04609

In the winter, the headquarters of the national park is: Bar Harbor Chamber of Commerce, 2 Cottage Street, at the corner of Cottage and Main streets

Phone: 207-288-3338

Website: https://www.nps.gov/acad/index.htm

Accessibility website: https://www.nps.gov/acad/planyourvisit/accessibility.htm

Maine

Verbal Image

The state of Maine is said to occupy almost as many square miles as all the other states in New England combined. It is approximately 320 miles (just under 515 kilometers) from north to south and approximately 210 miles (just under 340 kilometers) wide from east to west, with these dimensions providing the state with a total area of greater than 33,200 square miles (just under 86,000 square kilometers).[1]

Maine is known as the Pine Tree State and has a sparsely populated and largely rural culture; as of its last count, its sixteen counties
had a population of almost 1,330,000. On a map, its east and west land
borders are almost perfectly straight lines, with a ballooning, raggedy
border to the north and a jagged, diagonal coastal border to the south.
This latter diagonal border slopes up from southwest to northeast.

Maine lies to the far northeast of the US and features its most
northly-facing Atlantic coastline. However, despite this geographic
status, it is far from being the most northerly border state in the US—
Alaska is, and we'll discuss it in the next chapter—and its northern
border remains below the curving 49th parallel. It can be said that its
neighbors are similarly drawn, and its longest borders are those with
the Canadian provinces of New Brunswick to the east and Quebec to
the north and northwest, with the tall, thin state of New Hampshire
being its western land border. Subsequently, its uppermost region is
farther north than the Canadian cities of Montreal or Quebec City.
Maine is also very close to the northern borders of Massachusetts.

Climate and Wildlife

Climatically, Maine's rural and wilder areas are possibly easier to
visit than those of many other states, as its seasons tend to be temperate and its environment less hazardous than many others. It is
also particularly famous for its spectacular leaf displays in fall and
even has foliage information online allowing you to judge the best
times to visit. That said, it can have dangerous winters, and you
should be wary of this. In addition, it can also get very humid, with
warm, clammy summers; rainy and moist springs; and cold, wet
winters making some visits uncomfortable.[2]

Temperature-wise, Maine's springs have an average temperature
around 41 F (around 5 C), a summer temperature averaging around
70 F (just over 21 C), and winter average temperatures of around 12
F (just over −11 C) during which snow falls mostly inland. Its state
record high is around 105 F (just over 40 C), although this was in
1911, and its record low temperature is around −50 F (just over −45

C), recorded in January 2009 in Big Black River at approximately 770 feet (around 235 meters) high. The state's average annual rainfall and snowfall is just above 75 inches (just over 1,900 millimeters). However, Acadia sees fewer of these flurries, with an average snowfall of around 60 inches (just over 1,500 millimeters). The best news for those visiting Acadia, however, is that Maine's annual average of slightly more than one hundred clear days with sunshine is at its highest along the coastline, which is well known for its long, dry summer days.

Maine's wildlife also reflects its largely rural countryside and abundant coastline, and it is particularly well known for birds such as the chickadee, rare snowy owls, and a wide range of birds of prey such as peregrine falcons and hawks, as well as its whale population, porcupines, wild coon cats, and moose, the latter of which is the state animal. Moose are particularly abundant in Maine, with its state government claiming that it has more moose per mile than almost any other state—it said to have more than seventy-five thousand moose, a number second only to Alaska. Along the coastline of Maine, you'll also find whales, seals, puffins, spring warblers, sea ducks, and the sea animal that the state is perhaps best known for: lobsters. However, visitors to the coast should also be aware of blackflies from about mid-May through mid-June and mosquitoes particularly during the warm and humid parts of spring or during the wettest conditions, and travelers are advised to take protection.

Maine's plant life also reflects its largely temperate and rural environment, with New England Acadian trees, plentiful fruit bushes, and abundant broadleaf and mixed forests of largely mixed oaks on its northeastern coastline. Most notably, Maine is said to produce over 90 percent of the US blueberry crop.

Acadia National Park

Verbal Image
Acadia National Park (Acadia NP) is located in the southeast of Maine and is divided into three parts, two of which are on islands just

off the coast of Maine and the third of which is on a peninsula jutting south from the mainland. Acadia is over 250 miles (just a little over 400 kilometers) from Boston, Massachusetts, its nearest large city in the US, and around 50 miles (just a little over 80 kilometers) from Bangor, Maine. The headquarters of the park is located on Eagle Lake Road, off Route 233, in the town of Bar Harbor.[3]

The main part of Acadia and the area that forms its largest single landmass is Mount Desert Island and its small sub-islands, which were first charted by the French cartographer Samuel de Champlain in 1604. The French name of this island, Isles de Monts Desert, roughly translates into English as the "island of barren mountains" and was so called because the cold granite of its highlands was found to have little soil or vegetation growing on it. Open ocean lies just to the south of the national park, although an archipelago to its north and east shelters its upper shores from the worst ocean storms the Atlantic has to offer.

The national park takes up over half the island's landmass, with the major parts being to the northeast and southwest of the island, including part of the coastline. The island itself is the largest in Maine, at almost 110 square miles (almost 285 square kilometers) or 15 miles long by 8 miles across. On a map, it approximates the shape of a tall human skull, which is divided partially in two by a long, thin channel finishing in a bay.

Geographically, Mount Desert Island is only a few hundred yards off a stretch of rugged coastline, is connected by a road bridge to the mainland, and is thus relatively easy to access via automobile. By contrast, the sub-islands that also form this section of the national park are to the southeast of this main island; are more remote, wilder, and less inhabited; and can only be accessed by sea. As a result, these sub-islands are far less developed or visited than the main inland areas of Mount Desert Island.

The second-largest part of Acadia can be found on the smaller but no less important Isle au Haut, which roughly translates as "high island," and its small sub-island. This island is farther out into the

Atlantic Ocean, lies to the southwest of Mount Desert Island, is relatively small at just over twelve miles high and 8,000 acres (just over 32 square kilometers), and has a permanent population of less than one hundred.[4] It is shaped like a rough and angled trapezium, and the national park takes up the great majority of its landmass, with most of it being in the south part of the island. In terms of access, Isle au Haut can only be reached by seacraft and is generally less inhabited and has fewer services than Mount Desert Island.

The Schoodic Peninsula is the only part of Acadia on the mainland and is home to the National Park Service's training center, which is based in the former US Navy base NSGA Winter Harbor. The peninsula is the smallest part of Acadia, being only just over 2,500 acres (just over 10 square kilometers) in area, and it is located less than 5 miles to the northeast of Mount Desert Island. The part of the peninsula with the national park is sparsely populated, even less so than Isles des Monts Desert, and this population fluctuates according to seasons and visitors. It is also far from urban areas. In appearance, it is more rugged, wilder, and relatively flatter than the two island parts of Acadia, with the highest point being Schoodic Head with its stunning views of the coastline.

Acadia NP gets its name from the term used by French fishermen and traders in their description of the area given to European monarch Henry IV and is derived from the American Indian Mi'kmaq word *akadie* or *cadie*. This translates as "a piece of land." From this American Indian name, it is thought that early French visitors repronounced the word "l'Acadie."

As is typical of Maine, Acadia has largely rocky beaches and granite peaks, it is largely forested, and its climate is guided largely by the vast Atlantic Ocean to its east and south. This Atlantic weather also makes the park a wet area to visit, as it is second only to the Pacific Northwest in the US for rain throughout year. In the winter and early spring, Acadia is also prone to occasional ice storms, and fog can be frequent from June through August, although this can be stunning especially when viewed from above on its mountain peaks.

Nowadays, popular activities in Acadia include walking, cross-country skiing, and snowshoeing—more accessible versions of cross-country skiing and snowshoeing can be done on the park's carriage roads—mountain biking, snowmobiling, ice and regular fishing, dog sledding and skijoring, hiking, relaxing on or swimming along the coastal and lakeside beaches, boat cruises, viewing peregrine falcons and raptors, ranger-led tours, and evening amphitheater education programs. The programs led by the park rangers run from mid-May to mid-October, and Acadia also runs children's and family-focused programs.

Many of the most interesting activities and programs in the park are linked to the park's animal and plant life. For instance, there are ranger-led bird walks from spring to mid-fall and seal-spotting boat tours and whale-watching trips can be taken from Bar Harbor. And, of course, many visitors time their vacations to see the leaves turning color from September to their peak in mid-October.

For those who enjoy winter sports, local communities have ski equipment sales and rentals, but bear in mind that the park has banned snowshoeing or dogs on cross-country ski tracks. Also, you should bear in mind that the park disallows fat-tire bicycles on smoother parts of carriage roads, snowmobiles are not allowed on carriage roads except east of Eagle Lake to connect to Park Loop Road, and towing sledders or skiers are banned throughout. A full list of prohibitions is advertised by the park on its website.

Getting Around Acadia

Because of its protected status and isolated communities, there are perhaps unsurprisingly no airports in Acadia NP itself. Once in Acadia, if you want to travel to the Mount Desert Island or the Schoodic Peninsula, you can ride the Island Explorer shuttle bus for free from almost the end of June through early October. The bus is more accessible than most and has a wheelchair lift, and it is stated that it is ADA compliant. This bus will have routes to Bar Harbor; Northeast Harbor and Southwest Harbor, which are on Mount

Desert Island; and the Schoodic Peninsula. Once in Acadia on Mount Desert Island, there is a Park Loop Road that is somewhere over twenty-five miles long. Caution should be taken when leaving your vehicle when driving on this road, though, as the road has no shoulder.

When you visit Acadia outside traditional tourist seasons, travel in the park gets harder no matter what your access needs. Consequently, for safety's sake, all but two sections of Park Loop Road close to public traffic altogether between the beginning of December and mid-April, or when there are major storms. Generally speaking, these storms will roll in from the Atlantic or the Arctic during the winter. Alternatively, those traveling to Schoodic Peninsula can enter Acadia via US Coastal Route 1, or between the Schoodic Peninsula, Bar Harbor, and Winter Harbor, where there is a ferry service to the main section of the park.

Getting to the more remote Isle au Haut is more challenging than getting to the rest of Acadia for people with access issues. Its only regular means of entry is a ferry that goes from the town of Stonington on the mainland to the Isle au Haut Town Landing. The good news is this ferry service goes all year round, and you can ride it in the more tumultuous winter months. What is more, from around mid-June through late September, the ferry also stops at the Duck Harbor Boat Landing on the island.

When you're away from your automobile, Acadia has two wheelchair-accessible carriages based at Wildwood Stables on Mount Desert Island, with each carriage being capable of carrying two wheelchairs and four non-wheelchair passengers. These carriages were provided by Friends of Acadia and the Shelby Cullom Davis Foundation in 1998, are generally now used on the park's carriage roads, and can be booked from late May (Memorial Day to be precise) through mid-October (Columbus Day to be precise). You can get more information about these carriages and make bookings via Wildwood Stables, although I would advise contacting them at least a month in advance, if not more, before you visit, as bookings can't be guaranteed (phone: 877-276-3622 or https://acadiahorses .com/).

Acadia has forty-five miles (over 72 kilometers) of carriage roads for walkers, horses, and bicycles, some of which are largely accessible for those with mobility access issues, including those with wheelchairs. They are also largely friendly to visitors with vision loss. A local voluntary association, Friends of Acadia's Carriage Roads Endowment, works to make these roads accessible to people with mobility issues, although it is advised that these roads are more accessible via motorized wheelchairs than manual ones.

I'd advise you to check the condition of these carriage roads with rangers before you start planning your day routes, as a number of them are steep and uneven or lined with stones or gravel. I would also advise being with someone when you're walking these roads, and it may also be prudent to know safe exit points from your route, particularly if you have medical needs.

As with many other parks, Acadia's trails are generally less accessible than their carriage roads. This being said, visitors with and without access needs I have spoken to often say that Acadia's trails in the main area of the park, particularly Mount Desert Island, are largely user-friendly to people with most access needs if they are cautious. This is because the hard rock often makes for a stable underfoot passage.

The following points along the trails are reported to have accessible sightseeing areas: Wild Gardens of Acadia's Hemlock Path; Sieur de Monts's Jesup Path, although this is narrow in places; Intertidal Zone; Jordan Pond, although you should check with rangers about the safety of this area as there are a number of inaccessible stretches of the trail; Cadillac Mountain, which has a largely accessible trail leading up to it; Schoodic Point, which has largely accessible parking at scenic areas; and Thunder Hole, which has a largely accessible viewing ramp, restrooms, and walkway.

However, Acadia NP advises visitors to be very cautious on or to avoid the following paths if you have mobility access needs or vision loss, as they can be hazardous particularly in tough weather: Beech Cliff Trail where it reaches out from Echo Lake, Beehive Trail, Cadillac Mountain West Face Trail where it reaches out from Bubble Pond, Jordan Cliff Trail, Ladder Trail to Dorr Mountain, Perpendicular Trail on Mansell Mountain, and the ominously named Precipice Trail.

In addition, for those with breathing problems, you should be aware that Acadia has high levels of pollution and ozone, with studies in the past few years showing it has among the highest levels of pollution in New England. Before and during your visit, I would advise you to check on air quality by phoning the local ozone information line (phone: 207-288-3338). There is also information on Acadia's website about pollution and dangerous weather.

In common with other national parks, service dogs or sight-guiding dogs are allowed on parks and trails, as well as in the visitor centers and campsites when they are open to the public. However, all service animals must be controlled and leashed during your visits. Furthermore, you should be aware that domestic pets and emotional support animals are banned from Sand Beach, Echo Lake Beach, campsites on Isle au Haut, ladder trails, all of Acadia's public buildings, and lake areas and should not be brought along to ranger activities.

Acadia's Facilities

Acadia has numerous and largely accessible visitor centers, which are open outside the park's colder months, and many have parking spaces that are marked with access symbols. As with all places in the US, you'll need an accessibility sign or license plate on your automobile to use the accessible parking spaces.

Examples of accessible visitor centers include **Hulls Cove Visitor Center** just off ME 3, which has a largely accessible entrance, access lift, restrooms, theater, and bookstore; **Cadillac Mountain's Summit Center**, which has a largely accessible entrance, parking, and restrooms for those with mobility issues; **Jordan Pond House**, which has a largely accessible gift shop, restaurant, and restrooms, although you'll need to ask about getting access when you're there; Thunder Hole, which has a largely accessible information area, outside restrooms, and parking, although you should be aware the restrooms have no running drinking water and you may need assistance to get in; **Sieur de Monts Nature Center**, which has a largely accessible entrance and restrooms and is the base for mostly level trails for visitors with mobility issues; **Schoodic Education and Research Center**, which has a largely accessible entrance and restrooms; the park's Welcome Center outside winter and the park's headquarters in winter, the latter of which is in the Bar Harbor Chamber of Commerce and said to have a largely accessible entrance, restrooms, and water fountain.

Acadia also has a number of museums. Among the most popular museums in Acadia are:

- **The George B. Dorr Museum of Natural History** at 105 Eden Street, Bar Harbor, ME 04609. Phone: 207-288-5015. This is in the original headquarters of Acadia NP and is now a part of the College of the Atlantic.

- **The Abbe Museum** at 26 Mount Desert Street, PO Box 286, Bar Harbor, ME 04609. Phone: 207-288-3519 or e-mail: angela@abbemuseum.org. This museum focuses on American Indian history and culture.

- **Sieur de Monts Spring in Acadia NP** at 49 Sweetwater Circle, Bar Harbor, ME 04609.

- **The Bar Harbor Oceanarium** at 1351 State Route 3, Bar Harbor, ME 04609. Phone: 207-288-5005.

- **The Wendell Gilley Museum** at PO Box 254, 4 Herrick Road, Southwest Harbor, ME 04679. Phone: 207-244-7555 or e-mail: info@wendellgilleymuseum.org.

- **The Great Harbor Maritime Museum** at 124 Main Street, Northeast Harbor, ME 04662. Phone: 207-276-5262.

- **Old School House Museum Mount Desert and Somesville Museum and Gardens** at 373 Sound Drive, Mount Desert, ME. Phone: 207-276-9323.

For those who want to enjoy Acadia's beaches or have picnics, Echo Lake, Sand Beach, and Ike's Point are largely accessible to the shoreline and have mostly accessible parking and restrooms, although they have less accessible changing areas for those with mobility issues. Other examples of areas that have official and largely accessible picnic areas include Bear Brook, Fabbri, Frazer Point, Schoodic Peninsula, Pretty Marsh, Seawall, and Thompson Island. These areas will have largely accessible parking, restrooms, grills, and picnic tables.

Depending on where you stay, you should also be aware of the hospitals if needed. On Mount Desert Island there is **Mount Desert Island Hospital** at 10 Wayman Lane, Bar Harbor ME 04609. To contact the hospital, phone: 207-288-5081 or find full details on their website: www.mdihospital.org. Outside Acadia, nearby hospitals include: **Maine Coast Memorial Hospital** (50 Union Street, Ellsworth ME 04605, phone: 207-664-5311 or try the website: www.mcmhospital.org) and **Eastern Maine Medical Center** (489 State Street, Bangor ME 04402, phone: 207-973-7000 or try https://northernlighthealth.org/Eastern-Maine-Medical-Center).

Lodges and Campgrounds

You should be aware that Acadia's campsites have accessible facilities but can be situated in remote areas, have quite basic facilities, and can have little light at night. Acadia's campsites include **Blackwoods Campground** on the east side of Mount Desert Island, which can be said to be closest to the major parts of Acadia, its carriage roads, and Bar Harbor. It has a dump station and twelve drive-in sites and accepts RVs. This is said to be a popular campsite as it is close to many of the park's facilities and so I'd advise that you make reservations several months in advance. The campsite is open May through October. Phone: 877-444-6777 or find it on the following website: www.recreation .gov. **Seawall Campground** is on the west side of Mount Desert Island and is said to be less crowded than Blackwoods. This campground has space for RVs, five drive-in and five walk-in spaces, one group space, and a dump station. Seawall is open from late May through September. Phone: 877-444-6777, and it can be found on the following website: www.recreation.gov. **Schoodic Woods Campground** is on Schoodic Peninsula and is the newest campground in Acadia, with more modern facilities such as water and electric hookups. This is said to be a new site where much of the access is still developing. **Duck Harbor Campground** on Isle au Haut is much wilder than those on the peninsula or Mount Desert Island and can only be reached by sea. I'd strongly advise you to plan your trip to this campsite carefully before considering camping there. To find out about this campsite, contact Acadia's headquarters for more information.

Acadia administers park passes for camping, vehicle access, and so forth from Blackwoods Campground, Hulls Cove Visitor Center, Park Loop Road Entrance Station, Seawall Campground, Schoodic Woods Campground, Thompson Island Information Center, and Village Green Park, the latter of which is located in Bar Harbor. I would strongly advise you to contact Acadia headquarters for more information at least a month before you arrive, to plan your stay and discuss access (phone: 207-288-3338). As with all these sites, I'd particularly advise checking on opening times and dates on their websites before you book your visit, as seasonal opening times can vary radically. One thing you should also be aware of is that you aren't allowed to backcountry camp; that is to say, you can't camp in the Acadian wild as its environment is too fragile.

Learning Programs and Tours

The park offers a rolling schedule of tours and educational programs on topics such as local wildlife, fauna, the environment, and American Indian culture at Bar Harbor Chamber of Commerce, Cadillac Mountain Gift Shop, Jordan Pond Gift Shop, LL Bean in Freeport, Mount Desert Town Office, Northeast Harbor, Schoodic Institute, Rockefeller Hall in its Welcome Center, and Southwest Harbor and Tremont Chamber of Commerce. The information about and topics of these ranger programs change frequently, according to the season, and can be situated at sea as well as in the park's landmass.

These ranger-led education programs run from mid-May through mid-October, and a list of programs and booking are on Acadia's website (www.nps.gov/acad/planyourvisit/events.htm). As always, I'd advise contacting rangers directly at least a month before you plan to visit to explain your access needs. You should note that the accessibility of a number of Acadia's ranger-led boat cruises varies for people with mobility issues at different times of day. In particular, sea-based programs are felt to be better at high tide as they involve boarding ramps to get to these boats.

In these museums, visitors are often able to touch a number of the exhibits, with museum staff and local College of the Atlantic students also leading programs and interactive activities for individuals, schools, and regular groups of visitors. A number of the museums located on Mount Desert Island are also on bus routes, although you should check with the museum beforehand to check on public transport and accessible parking.

Finally, Acadia offers different general and bespoke services to support learning for **visitors with access needs**. In particular, **visitors with hearing loss** can request ASL interpretation for any of Acadia's face-to-face tours or programs, and large-print and assisted-listening devices can be arranged for park programs. For some programs, particularly those based in the visitor centers, there is also the possibility of audio description. I'd advise you to contact the relevant visitor center and rangers when you book onto a tour to request a service, at least a month before you plan to visit.

Similarly, **visitors with vision loss** can ask for an accessible version of the park's orientation video via phone or e-mail. You can also buy a recorded audio tour from Hulls Cove Visitor Center, which contains a verbal-imaging narrative of much of the Park Loop Road, Somes Sound, and Mount Cadillac's Summit. You can also get a fifteen-minute narrative of the park from the Welcome Video at the Hulls Cove Visitor Center. To get a Brailled introduction to Acadia, contact Hulls Cove Visitor Center or download a soft copy of the Braille Ready Format (.BRF) introduction to Acadia from its website.

Featured Online Learning

Acadia offers a number of school programs, and among its most popular and enduring are its literacy and language arts and social studies programs on the local American Indian cultures in Acadia. For instance, one of the programs the park offers is "Passamaquoddy History and Culture: A Traveling Teaching Kit," which is suitable for third-grade through fifth-grade students and can be requested by local schools. The kit is largely accessible as it has a high degree of interactivity. If you would like to borrow it for your classes, let the park administrators and rangers know you have students with access needs when you request the kit. Information on this program can be found on the following website: https:// www.nps.gov/teachers/classrooms/passamaquoddy-history-culture -a-traveling-teaching-kit.htm. When you request this program, you'll also have to arrange a collection time.

Specialized Access

Beyond these highly specific services, if you have any access needs, I'd advise letting the rangers know about them when you book your tour or program, at least a month before you plan to visit. However, if you want to use one of these services, I'd advise you to contact the park at least a month before you visit, as they will need to plan.

For all these services, phone: 207-288-8832 or alternatively e-mail: acadia_information@nps.gov. You can also find more on accessibility in Acadia from the park's accessibility web page (https://www.nps.gov/acad/planyourvisit/upload/Accessibility Guide.pdf). Alternatively, you can find more information on the following websites: https://friendsofacadia.org/what-we-do/trails-and -carriage-roads/wheelchair-access/ or https://www.outsideonline .com/2318861/best-national-parks-those-disabilities#close.

DENALI, ALASKA

Address: PO Box 9, Denali Park, AK 99755
Phone: 907 683 9532
Website: https://www.nps.gov/dena/index.htm
Accessibility website: https://www.nps.gov/dena/index.htm

Alaska

Verbal Image

It is almost impossible to encapsulate the vastness and wilderness of Alaska in a short description. Space-wise, and at its longest, Alaska is over 1,400 miles (over 2,280 kilometers) and more than 2,200 miles (just under 3,640 kilometers) wide. By area, it is the largest state in the US with a landmass that is just over 570,640 square miles (just under 1,478,000 square kilometers). Despite this vastness, it is only lightly inhabited, with a total population of fewer than 742,000 people, many of whom are in the largest urban areas, such as Anchorage and Fairbanks. This makes the rest of the state wilderness, with wildlife roaming unhindered, as it has done for as long as nature has existed in this area. For this reason, Alaska is known as the Last Frontier.[1]

Alaska is also, of course, by far the most northerly state in the US and does not touch any other part of the US on any of its borders—its closest neighbors are Canada and then Russia. The shape of Alaska is bulbous: its eastern border is a largely straight line where it meets Canada, and to the west it is largely a huge, raggedy coastal boundary line stretching out into the Bering Straits and the Arctic.

To the south of the main body of the state, there is also a tendril of land that droops down along the western coast of Canada. This strip of Alaska is mostly made up of islands off the coast, which hug the shore as it follows a vast swath of North American coastline as seen on a map. Through this tendril, Alaska also appears to block what must be comfortably two-thirds of the coastline of North America above Washington State. To the west of its southern borders, Alaska also has a long line of islands that stretch far into the northern Pacific in a curving patterned line that looks like a wasp sting.

Alaska's geography also largely defines its cultural as well as physical distance from the rest of the US, something that draws many people looking for an alternative lifestyle to the hustle and bustle of the rest of the country. South and east of its main land-mass, Alaska is bordered by the Canadian provinces of Yukon and British Columbia, which are also largely wilderness. To the west, it almost touches the largely barren Russian state of Siberia, just across the short passage of the Bering Straits. In this respect, it is closer to Russia and the shores of eastern Asia and Asia's outlying islands, like Japan, than it is to most of the US. This defines so much of its culture as unique and beyond that of other Americans.

Climate and Wildlife

Climatically, Alaska is an exciting but often hazardous place to visit.[2] The state has dark, harsh winters with few hours of light and extreme summers with up to twenty-four-hour daylight from its central regions and up to the north. More particularly, daylight ranges from nineteen and a half hours to twenty-four hours of sunshine during the year's longest day and between six hours to no sunlight at all on the shortest day—in parts, no sunlight appears for more than two months of the year.

This lack of light means that Alaska is also not a state to visit for glorious weather, as it only has sixty-one clear days of sunshine per year, has average temperatures of just under 27 F (around –3 C), summer temperatures just over 52 F (just over 11 C), and winter average temperatures of over 2.5 F (just over –16 C). The state's record high was some time ago, in June 1915, when records reached around 100 F (just under 38 C) in Fort Yukon near its Canadian border. Its record low temperature was more recent and around an eye-watering –80 F (around –62 C) in January 1971 at Prospect Creek Camp, although admittedly this was at a height of around 1,100 feet. Alaska also has moderate humidity, with an average annual snowfall of around 48 days and just under 75 inches (almost 1,900 millimeters) and an average annual rainfall of just over 22 inches (more than 570 millimeters). This makes its atmosphere feel colder even when the sun shines, although its wilderness air is good, as in the wilderness it has little pollution.

Alaska's wildlife is unique in the US and is particularly diverse, with many species that don't exist in any other parts of the country. This diversity is essentially a product of its vastness, its emptiness, and an exceptional environment that is only rarely, and even then lightly touched by human hands. Among its most important fauna are the wonderfully named pine grosbeaks, northern goshawks, black and grizzly bears, gawky moose, and caribou. It is also home to the famous Dall sheep, packs of wolves who rule its wilderness like monarchs of the snow, collared pika, red foxes, snowshoe hares, Arctic ground and red squirrels, ptarmigan, Arctic warblers, and the iconic golden eagle and Canada jay.

Offshore, Alaska is known for natural whale-watching shows, including its spectacular humpbacks and orcas, which often fly from the ocean in one of nature's most spectacular displays. By contrast, in its soft freshwater rivers, it is famous for the spawning of sockeye salmon that are a particularly tasty treat for its bears and make it a magnet for those who love fishing.

Denali National Park

Verbal Image

The entrance to Denali National Park[3] (Denali NP) is clearly inland from the Gulf of Alaska and a little under 240 miles (just over 340 kilometers) and a few degrees northwest of the coastal city of Anchorage by highway AK-3. However, given the size of Alaska as a state, it is also still in the southern region and what seems to be in the vertical center of the state. Just as important, the park is also just over 120 miles (just over 195 kilometers) from the home rule city of Fairbanks, also on AK-3, which itself is to the northeast of Denali and closer to the border with Canada.

Denali NP is formed of a single landmass that is, roughly speaking, a small preserve to the southwest that climbs and expands as it rises to the northeast. The general shape of the park is a little like that of an anvil balancing on a small block to its southwest corner. The feature that regularizes this shape is its perfectly flat northern border and jagged right angles that form its outer edges.

The imposing Alaska Mountain Range that Denali NP is a part of forms the southeastern and much of the eastern border of the national park. The rest of the park, including wild rivers, the mountain valley, and flatter woodland and the rough open preserve, runs off these mountains to the southwest and west and forms the majority of the park from above.

With its famous peak rising to just over 20,300 feet (just under 6,200 meters) tall, enormous glaciers filling its valleys and canyons, and sweeping backcountry, Denali NP is home to and named after the highest mountain in the US. The name Denali roughly translates as "the high one" in the local Athabascan language, with its name being changed from Mount McKinley to reflect its older, more traditional American Indian culture in 2015.

Following its previous estimated measurement, the truer altitude of Denali was established in 2015 using GPS systems from orbiting satellites in the same year as its name was changed. This provided a much more accurate height than had previously been achieved through conventional means. Importantly, the park incorporates more than six million primitive acres designed to be ruled by animal and plant life rather than human cultivation.

Geographically, Denali is situated on an important fault line, a crease in the earth's thin surface formed by large areas of rock pushing up on either side of it, thus creating the rugged land surface. Alaska as a whole is susceptible to these fault lines and is in one of North America's most vulnerable areas, with geological plate boundaries just off the southern coast of Alaska that stretch out into the Bering Straits. This fault line forms both beauty and significant dangers, as Alaska is part of one of the US's most dangerous earthquake zones. In 1964, in particular, Alaska logged what is thought to be the second-largest earthquake ever recorded just off its southern coast.

Getting Around Denali

Denali NP is unusual for a national park as it only has a single, restricted-use road that is almost 120 miles long. It's important to understand that, generally speaking, you can also only drive your own automobile on the first fifteen miles of this road. After that, you'll have to travel the remaining ninety-plus miles on the many concession buses that are licensed to travel through Denali.

The concession buses can be taken from the Denali Bus Depot, which is not far from the entrance to the park and has a large parking lot, a good number of which are spaces for large automobiles, such as recreational vehicles (RVs). The bus depot also links to buses going elsewhere in Alaska and other nearby public transport stops.

The concession buses shuttle visitors to the main visitor centers in the park and sites of interest, like the dog kennels for local sled teams. At the time of writing, these buses included the Savage River Shuttle, the Riley Loop Shuttle, and the Sled Dog Demonstration Shuttle, which operated from late May through mid-September. As with everything at the park, it's best to check with Denali NP about the precise dates if you are thinking of visiting. Contact the office via phone: 907-683-9532.

For **visitors with mobility issues**, concession buses and resort shuttle buses often have wheelchair lifts, although it's best to ask when booking tickets at Denali Bus Depot if you need this facility, as it isn't guaranteed. I'm afraid you can't ask ahead of your visit as buses constantly change, and it isn't known what bus will be available at any given time. Buses generally also have front bus seats reserved for **visitors with access needs** and a stool to get onto buses for people with mobility issues. The concession buses stop at restrooms roughly every hour and a half as they travel around the park, and the bathrooms they stop at are largely accessible.

As you travel into the park on the park road, you'll find that the ground around the main park road is much rougher, and of course there is little or no sidewalk or pathway, so it will be less accessible for people with mobility issues. However, around the park entrance, there are fewer issues of access. There are many good reasons why it's best to use the shuttle buses in Denali National Park if you have access needs, but in addition there are three sound environmental and safety reasons why it's a particularly good decision.

First, and as you would expect, the road travels through valleys and then upward into the Alaska Mountain Range and can get to more than 4,000 feet (above 1,200 meters) above sea level. This makes it particularly treacherous especially in difficult weather, and it takes an experienced driver to navigate the surface safely and correctly, although as always this isn't guaranteed even for trained and experienced drivers. Nature will occasionally throw a curveball. Second, Denali's wildlife roams freely over the roads, and automobiles need to be particularly careful not to harm the animals or allow the animals to cause harm to those in automobiles. Third, as you'd expect from a wilderness area, the National Parks Service doesn't want more traffic in the park than is necessary. The park particularly doesn't want to provide unnecessary extra parking facilities that take away from its primitive wilderness or generate extra pollution.

This being said, **visitors with severe mobility issues** and who find it too difficult to ride buses can apply for a road travel permit. This will take time to process, so I'd recommend contacting the park at least two months before your visit. If you are granted a permit, you can travel in a private automobile on the parts of Denali Park Road that are normally banned for regular automobiles. The application form can be requested via a link on the accessibility page of the park's website: https://www.nps.gov/dena/planyourvisit/accessibility.htm.

Denali's Facilities

For many of the warmer, lighter months of the year, the Denali Bus Depot is usually your first stop in the park. The depot is open from 5 a.m. to 7 p.m. daily to buy tickets for travel around the park and for information on bus departures, as well as to get coffee, sodas, food, and so forth. In addition, many of the park's more tourist-like and learning tours can be arranged from here, and there is information about the rest of the park and its more backcountry centers and activities. Again, depending on the time of sunlight and tourist seasons, the hours of tours and the amount of information will most likely vary.

From the bus depot, you can also get tickets and check into campgrounds until around 7 p.m. in the summer, although past 7 p.m., you can do check-ins at Riley Creek Mercantile store at Riley Creek Campsite, which usually is open until later in the evening. Riley Creek Campsite is actually the first campsite in Denali NP, close to the park entrance, and you'll see it before arriving at the depot. Again, I'd strongly advise that you get in touch with the park before you arrive, explaining your access needs to get the precise times for when you visit or to arrange for a park ranger to support you.

Importantly, Denali NP has a number of main information and education centers for visitors; each has access facilities and provides advice about access to the rest of the park and wilderness areas. Close to the entrance of the park is a complex of resources, which includes the **Denali Visitor Center**, which is at Mile 1.5 Denali Park Road, Denali Park, AK 99755; in the same complex is **Denali Bus Depot**, which includes what is referred to as the "**Wilderness Access Center**," and is at Mile 1.5 Denali Park Road, Denali Park, AK 99755; and the **Murie Science and Learning Center** at Mile 1.4 Denali Park Road, Denali Park, AK 99755.

Denali Visitor Center has borrowable wheelchairs, which are free to use but are not reservable, so their availability isn't guaranteed. The visitor center and the Denali Bus Depot are also largely paved from the parking lot to their different parts, although the path may slope in places. The bus depot and the visitor center also have buttons to open their front doors, benches and elevators inside and outside, and largely accessible bathrooms and a "family" bathroom. The water fountains and water-filling station are also largely accessible to **visitors who use wheelchairs**, and the Wilderness Access Center inside the bus depot has exhibits at wheelchair height.

In other parts of the park, along the Park Road, are other visitor centers, including **Toklat River Contact Station** at Mile 53, Denali Park Road, Denali Park, AK 99755; **Eielson Visitor Center** at Mile 66, Denali Park Road, Denali Park, AK 99755; and, off the Park Road, **Walter Harper Talkeenta Ranger Station** on B Street, Talkeetna, AK 99676. This latter visitor center is based some ways from Denali NP, more than two hours' drive away, and is open to issue climbing permits and provide orientations for climbers in the park. These centers have a single telephone contact point; phone: 907-683-9532.

The visitor centers and the dog kennels mostly have accessible spaces in their parking lots, although the size of these will vary and so you'll need to check with the park if you plan to bring an RV or larger automobile. As always, the number of spaces is limited and so can't be guaranteed. These centers and the kennels also have largely accessible theaters and amphitheaters, although seating isn't guaranteed, so you should again contact Denali NP about your access needs before you attend a program or talk.

Denali NP also has a number of day areas around its visitor centers and campgrounds. In these areas, you can have picnics and start your treks, and the great majority of these sites have at least some accessible parking spaces for automobiles with disability badges. In these sites, there are also at least a number of largely accessible bathrooms or bathroom stalls, and there are benches for those who need frequent rests. The pathways around these areas are also largely compacted gravel and therefore more accessible than rough paths or ground for people with mobility issues, as are the pathways around the campsites I list below.

If you need medical assistance in the park or you need permanent medical support, the following are medical centers or places that can be reached or that can provide remote treatment. It should be borne in mind that, given the vastness of the park, getting to these centers can be problematic. The medical centers include:

- **Canyon Clinic at Denali**. Address: Denali National Park, AK 99755. Phone: 907-683-4433.

- **Arctic Village Health Clinic**. Address: Arctic Village, AK 99722. Phone: 907-587-5229.

- **Stevens Village Clinic**. Address: Stevens Village, AK 99774. Phone: 907-478-7215.

- **Edith Kawagley Memorial Clinic**. Address: Akiak, AK 99552. Phone: 907-765-7125.

- **Cantwell Community Clinic**. Address: Cantwell, AK 99729. Phone: 907-768-2122.

- **US Air Force**. Address: 200 A Street, Clear, AK 99704. Phone: 907-585-6415.

- **Independence Park Medical**. Address: 9500 Independence Drive, Suite 900, Anchorage, AK 99507. Phone: 907-522-1341.

- **Women's Care of Alaska**. Address: C-205, 2741 Debarr Road, Anchorage, AK 99508. Phone: 907-279-2273.

Lodges and Campgrounds

Because Denali's temperatures and lighting can be extreme, if you feel you want comfort, it can be safer to stay in a nearby local commercial resort, as the weather and wildlife is potentially hazardous for all visitors. There is a chalet resort a manageable way from the park entrance, and it has a number of accessible chalet rooms that are compliant with the Americans with Disabilities Act. These rooms are limited in number, though, so I'd advise you to book at least three months in advance by telephone, explaining your access needs as you do so.

The resort also has a partly accessible shuttle bus that picks up and drops off guests at Denali's main visitor center and Denali Bus Depot with its Wilderness Access Center. You can also arrange transportation from the resort to the Denali Railroad Station and book non-park tours. However, I'm not going to talk about this more in this book, as it is my rule to be noncommercial in this book.

For those of you who'd prefer to camp, it's best to consider that the park's official campgrounds often have no electricity, and a number have no showers and so are not for the fainthearted. It should be noted that only Riley Creek Campground is open all year round, but most campgrounds have parking for those who get to drive there in a rugged automobile, and most have largely accessible bathrooms and dump stations. Likewise, it's important to note that all but Riley Creek Campground have no shower facilities and electricity.

Campground fees for Riley Creek Campground vary during summer, fall, and spring, although at the time of writing there was free camping in the winter months. Other campgrounds can only be booked from May until September, and reservations can be made in the December of the year before you visit. You will need to book camping online via concessioners who manage the campgrounds, and I'd advise you to book well in advance if you have access needs (website: https://www.reservedenali.com/). The park also advertises that Senior Pass and Access Pass holders get 50 percent off camping fees. For more information on camping, e-mail denali_info@nps .gov or phone 907-683-9532.

The campgrounds are as follows: **Riley Creek Campground** is, as I wrote above, close to the park entrance; has the most facilities of all of the campgrounds, including electricity and showers; and has paved level areas around and a largely accessible amphitheater where it hosts talks. Unless you want to go full wilderness and if you like to smell sweet in the morning, this is perhaps the safest option. This campground also has a concession store—where the bathrooms and showers can be found—and can be reached relatively easily from the bus depot. The address is PO Box 9, Denali Park, AK 99755. **Teklanika River Campground** has flat camping areas and paths with few slopes. The address is Mile 29, Denali Park Road, Denali Park, AK 99755. **Wonder Lake Campground** is closest to Denali Mountain, can only be reached by the concession bus, and has park staff on site, so it is manageable if you need support and assistance during your visit. It also has a single accessible bathroom. The address is Mile 85, Denali Park Road, Denali Park, AK 99755. **Savage River Campground** is accessible to automobiles and has accessible parking spaces. It also has staff on site and largely accessible bathrooms. The address is Mile 14 Denali Park Rd., Denali Park, AK 99755. **Sanctuary River Campground** can only be reached by bus and is what can be called rough camping, as it has rocky, uneven ground. The address is Mile 22, Denali Park Road, Denali Park, AK 99755. **Igloo Creek Campground** can also only be reached by bus and has only one accessible bathroom. The address is Mile 35, Denali Park Road, Denali Park, AK 99755.

Learning Programs and Tours

Programs led by the park rangers usually start around March, when the days get warmer and lighter and it is safer to be outdoors, and many of the tours can take advantage of pathways that are more accessible. There are also a number of activity-type tours with rangers traveling via dogsled, cross-country skiing, and snowshoeing. Depending on the nature of the tour and your confidence levels, these programs can be challenging but rewarding for those with access needs, although I'd check with the center before you decide whether to book these or not. You can also visit Denali's kennels and learn about the breeding and use of sled dogs, with the option of asking a ranger to walk with you through the dog yard if you have mobility issues.

The chalet resort I wrote about above, the visitor centers, and some campsites also have a program of talks in their theaters and amphitheaters and on concession buses. Depending on the venues, these talks can start in May at the earliest and finish in September and are themed on the geography, geology, fauna, and flora of Denali NP, although this varies according to the venue. I'd advise contacting the park at least a month or so before you visit, to check on the appropriateness of the program and to arrange specialist access facilities. There is also information online for all these talks: https://www.nps.gov/dena/planyourvisit/ranger-talks.htm.

For **visitors with hearing loss**, Denali Visitor Center, Toklat River Visitor Center, and Eielson Visitor Center have videos, such as "Heartbeats of Denali" and "Across Time and Tundra," and audio exhibits all with closed captions. The screening room in the Eielson Visitor Center also has an induction loop system for hearing aids with T-Switch. In these and other visitor centers with Denali NP exhibits, education programs, and tours, you can borrow assisted-listening devices or neck loops for hearing aids with T-Switches.

Borrowable manuscripts of many of the videos that are shown in the centers and some tours are available on request from a ranger or officer during your visit, although it's best to check on specific tours before you visit to see if these are available. Assisted-listening devices, such as neck loops, and regular headphones can also be borrowed for audio tours during your visit to the centers. Visitors can also ask for ASL translation for tours or talks, although you'll need to request a signer sometime before you visit; I'd advise you to contact the park at least a month in advance. Send an e-mail via the following page: https://www.nps.gov/dena/contacts.htm or phone 907-683-2294 or 907-733-2231.

Tours on the concession buses can also arrange ASL, but you'll need to contact the concessioner directly to arrange this. They advertise that you'll need to contact them two weeks in advance, but I would advise contacting at least a month in advance of booking your ticket, if possible. Check the following two websites for contact details and details of the tours: https://www.nps.gov/dena/planyourvisit/bus-tours.htm and https://www.reservedenali.com/; or phone 866-761-6629.

Borrowable Braille information on the park and some learning materials for **visitors with vision loss** is available at Denali Visitor Center and the Denali Bus Depot/Wilderness Access Center. The visitor center also has audio description for its film *Heartbeats of Denali* via a borrowable listening device. Other Denali NP information can also be converted to multiple formats if you request it beforehand, but I would strongly advise contacting the park at least a month in advance to let them know your needs.

Most of the visitor centers also have a number of touchable exhibits and pieces on tours or during talks; however, it should be borne in mind that tours and talks can change, and pieces cannot be guaranteed. However, the ranger-led tours are often said to purposely include multisensory experiences for visitors and include pieces that can be passed around to all visitors during the presentations.

The sled dog kennels can also arrange a ranger to support you in the dog yard, and this is particularly advisable even for the most independent visitor, as the sled dogs have a habit of rearing up. Also, it should be noted that you'll need to be cautious with service animals and particularly seeing-eye dogs when you visit the kennels.

Online, the park's official brochure is available in a variety of formats, including text-only and audio-only.

Featured Online Learning

For schoolchildren and adults who can't make it to the park physically, Denali NP offers a full distance-learning education program, and at the time of writing, this included a number of Zoom sessions that could be signed up for. These sessions can change, and you'll also need to book in advance for the live session, so I'd advise you book at least a month in advance, if possible. Information about these programs and the link for booking can all be found on the following web page: https://www.nps.gov/dena/learn/education/learning/index.htm.

Denali NP also has several online educational resources on its wildlife, geography, and natural history, including a dinosaur program. It also advertises a number of virtual tours and online videos, many of which have closed captions and one of which includes a tour by a group of **visitors with hearing loss** that includes ASL, at the time of writing. The resources are in PDF format and so can be zoomed into but may be restricted to screen readers for **visitors with vision loss** who use these devices. The educational material is on the following web page: https://www.nps.gov/dena/learn/education/education-resources.htm, and the online tours are at https://www.nps.gov/dena/learn/photosmultimedia/index.htm.

For further information about services, phone 907-683-9532 or use the e-mail contact form at https://www.nps.gov/dena/contacts.htm. You can also find more on Denali's accessibility web page: https://www.nps.gov/dena/planyourvisit/accessibility.htm.

EVERGLADES, FLORIDA

Address: 40001 State Road 9336, Homestead, FL 33034

Phone: 305-242-7700

Website: https://www.nps.gov/ever/index.htm

Accessibility website: https://www.nps.gov/ever/planyourvisit/
accessibility.htm

Florida

Verbal Image

It's apt that this chapter on the Everglades and Florida follows on from a chapter on Alaska, as you could not find two more different states. Whereas parts of Alaska are in darkness for parts of the year, Florida has sunshine almost all year round, which of course makes both states equally charming for different reasons. Both states are also at opposite sides and at the extreme north and south of North America and the US, although Florida is run close by the southern tip of Texas, both of which share a longitude with much of central Mexico.[1]

North to south, Florida is just under 450 miles long (just over 720 km) and just over 360 miles (just over 580 km) wide west to east. Although not the largest state in the country, Florida is large at over 65,700 square miles (which is over 170,300 square kilometers). At its base, Florida is an elegant, slowly bulging peninsula with a wide but short section stretching to the northwest of the peninsula above. This northwestern section, which is otherwise known as the Florida panhandle, borders Georgia and Alabama to the north of the state.

As it is mostly a peninsula with the Gulf of Mexico to the west, the Atlantic Ocean to the east, and the Caribbean Sea to its south, its coastline is vast and rough lined and, as a consequence, has variations in in climate and environment. The peninsula's shape is mainly made up of low-lying land gently curving outward from northeast to southwest. In addition to its geographical size, Florida has more than twenty-one million residents, with most living in its largest urban areas, such as Jacksonville and Miami, with Jacksonville being Florida's largest city.

Florida is also known as the Sunshine State, an apt name, given its subtropical climate. Environmentally, it is largely governed by the water surrounding it, and off its southern coast, Florida has the world's third-largest living coral reef system, and is designated as the US's only undersea preserve—there is more about this below. This gives Florida a particularly rich and highly diverse geography, with everything other than natural ice and glaciers and ski resorts.

Despite many areas of diversity, Florida is geographically flat, with the highest summit in the state, Sugarloaf Mountain, being only 312 feet (95 meters) above sea level—this is another opposite to Denali in Alaska. To highlight the lowness of its land, Britton Hill is the lowest state high point in the United States at 345 feet (105 meters). This lowest hill can be found in northern Walton County, near the town of Lakewood, Florida, just a few miles away from the border with Alabama.

All of this being said, figures alone don't paint a true picture of the state of Florida, and they undersell its human, environmental, and climatic diversity. Visitors to the state should enjoy Florida's cultural wealth, with too many interesting communities in its cities to describe in such a short chapter. In its rural areas to the north of the state, Florida also has farming communities famous for their warm-weather produce, and it is perhaps most famous for producing 70 percent of the US orange crop, which is mainly for juicing. In addition to its agriculture, Florida also has an impressive science, engineering, and tourist heritage, and is of course famous as a base for NASA's launchpad at Cape Canaveral and for Walt Disney World on the outskirts of the city of Orlando.

Climate and Wildlife

Perhaps unsurprisingly for a subtropical state surrounded by seas and ocean on three of its four sides, Florida is notorious for being both warm and wet. Although perhaps surprising to many, the state's wettest months are in the summer, when it records most of its annual 55 inches (1,397 millimeters) of rain, so prepare for this when you plan your visit. Despite this rain, it rarely ever reaches temperatures low enough to snow and at the time of writing had an average annual snowfall of 0 snowfall days with only 0.1 inches of snow on the ground.

Florida is also known to be hit by spectacular thunderstorms in the summer, particularly along its coastline on the Gulf of Mexico, and hurricanes and tornadoes in the autumn and winter. These storms are particularly severe on its Atlantic coastlines and nearby Caribbean waters. In fact, as I write this chapter and check on Florida, parts of the state are closed due to flooding from a current storm.[2]

Unlike the almost monsoon-like summer and autumn, the winter and spring in Florida are relatively dry and can be the most pleasant times to visit outside hurricane season. In this period, many people continue to swim off its shores, as the state is warmed constantly by the Gulf Stream currents, and enjoy the pure air that comes in off its coastline that gives Florida some of the least polluted atmosphere in the US.

As for its climate, Florida has an average temperature of over 70 F (around 21.5 C), with a summer average of over 80 F (which is around 27 C) and a winter average of just under 60 F (a little over 15 C). The record high temperature was around ninety years ago, in June 1931 at Monticello, when it reached 109 F (a little under 43 C). Its record low temperature was even longer ago, in February 1899 in Tallahassee, when it dropped to −2 F (around −19 C). Florida is also one of the wettest US states, with an average annual rainfall of just under 55 inches (which is around 1,385 millimeters).

This constantly warm, wet climate means that Florida's fauna is mostly that found in the subtropics elsewhere in the world, although Florida is said to be the only place where you will see alligators and crocodiles in the same environment. In addition to these spectacular hard-skinned dinosaurs, you can also find majestic birds such as roseate spoonbills, bald eagles, great blue herons, and pelicans flying low across sea waters; charming and less ferocious reptiles such as sea turtles; the unique West Indian manatee; and, farther out in the ocean, Atlantic bottlenose dolphins. Inland, you'll also be able to see bobcats, black bears, Florida panthers, armadillos, key deer, fox squirrels, and hundreds of species of butterflies.

Florida is no less famous for its amazing and often stunning plant life, which is also worth a mention. The state's most famous trees include oaks, bald cypresses, Florida maples, Florida and longleaf pines, and cycads. Similarly, its plants and bushes are also spectacular, and include the beautifully named black-eyed Susan, Chickasaw plum, coral honeysuckle, wild coffee, muhly grass, star anise, oakleaf hydrangea, firebush, southern magnolia, fern, spider-wort, native orchids made famous by the book *The Orchid Thief*, and the charismatic yucca.

Everglades National Park

Verbal Image
The Everglades National Park (Everglades NP) is at the southern tip of Florida's mainland and uniquely includes part of the ocean to its south as part of the national park—this is an exceptional subtropical

marine preserve and unrivaled in the US. Unusually for such a wild national park, the Everglades NP also touches the outer suburbs of the metropolitan areas of three large Floridian cities: Miami, to the northeastern borders of the park; Homestead, which is farther to the south of Miami and to the east of much of the park; and the appropriately named Everglades City, which is on the far northwestern tip of the Everglades.[3]

The Everglades NP is also close to other large cities in Florida, such as Fort Lauderdale, which is usually just over an hour's drive and a little under fifty miles via the Ronald Reagan Turnpike to the northeast of the park or just over fifty miles via FL-836 E and I-95 Express. A little closer, the city of Naples is usually just over forty minutes' drive or just over thirty-five miles (a little under sixty kilometers) northwest of Everglades City's entrance to the park via US-41. This route also takes you close to Florida's Gulf coastline.

The borders of the park reflect these three large, prominent cities and the ragged eastern edges work their way around the suburbs and outer limits of Miami and Homestead in particular, forming a bulging shape to its west until it meets the coastline of the Gulf of Mexico. To the south of the park, the sea border of Everglades marine preserve in Florida Bay is bordered itself to the southeast by the small islands that form the Florida Keys. The only straight borders of the Everglades are a right angle and a straight line where the national park meets the southern flat borders of Big Cypress National Preserve and other wild landmasses to the north.

The Everglades NP can be described at its widest point as a more than 1,500,000-acre, sixty-mile-wide river that flows slowly from north to south. This river takes the copious rainwaters of southern Florida to the surrounding warm ocean waters of the Gulf and the Atlantic. Given its size as the largest tropical wetlands in the US, it has areas of unique wilderness that have led to its designations as a UNESCO World Heritage Site, an International Biosphere Reserve, and the special designation of a Wetland of International Importance granted by the Cartagena Treaty. Within its boundaries, it has freshwater and saltwater marshes and huge expanses of wetland sawgrass, mangrove swamps, tropical hardwood islands known as hardwood hammocks, pine and cypress forests, and unique marine habitats off its coastline.[4]

A relatively young national park that was established in December 1947, the Everglades has around one million annual visitors. The area of the national park gets its name from early British explorers in Florida who saw wide expanses of sawgrass prairie and named them ever (for "eternal") glades (an old English word for "clearing in a woodland"). Similarly, the local American Indian Seminole community named the area Okeechobee, or "river of grass." This swamp and forest land is now home to a large number of animals and plant life and is said to have more than four hundred bird species.

Getting Around Everglades

Two main roads bisect the national park: Highway 41, which goes from Miami to Everglades City, west to east; and Highway 9336, which connects Homestead with the remote Flamingo Visitor Center at Florida Bay on the southern tip of the Florida mainland and which runs from northwest to southeast and has a small loop road partway along. However, these roads cover relatively little of the park's total area, and so many people rely on forms of travel that float or fly or hover on the waters through the sawgrass, and give another exciting reason to visit the Everglades NP.

Most forms of transport around the Everglades NP include boat and plane concessions and also the iconic hovering boats with large, powerful blades fixed to their rears. Many of the coastal concessioner boat tours are largely accessible to those with mobility access needs, and the boats are said to be able to accommodate those in wheelchairs.

Once away from your automobile, there are areas that can be traveled on maintained paths and boardwalks if you have mobility access needs—although I'd advise you to check on these before you plan to travel, as recent extreme weather conditions can change accessibility. For those visitors who prefer cycling, there are regular and electric bicycles around the Homestead and Miami park entrances, including electrical bicycles on the Shark Valley loop road, and the nearby visitor centers have concessioners who rent bicycles.

One trekking highlight of the area is the National Audubon Society's Corkscrew Swamp Sanctuary. This area has pinelands and cypress trees in thirteen thousand acres of wetlands. The forests are said to be around five thousand years old, but the oldest trees are thought to be around a mere seven hundred years old because many generations of trees have been destroyed by natural fires in the area. The sanctuary also has a largely accessible boardwalk that is over two miles long.

Shorter trails that are said to be the most accessible to those with mobility access needs, such as access for those in wheelchairs and mobility scooters, include the Bobcat Hammock, Pineland Trail, Mahogany Hammock Trail, Pa-hay-okee Overlook, Anhinga Trail, Gumbo Limbo Trail, and West Lake Trail. A number of these trails are near the visitor centers, have largely accessible parking and restrooms nearby, and are signed as accessible in large print for **visitors with visual impairment**—although the signs are not Brailled.

Apart from the private concession transport, there is relatively little public transport in the Everglades NP. However, there is a tram that conducts a fifteen-mile looping route around Shark Valley, which starts off close to the Miami entrance to the park. The tram also stops at an observation tower along the way, and the tower has a ramp. However, the Everglades NP advises that this is only partly accessible to **visitors with mobility access needs**, as the ramp is long and steep. In addition, for **visitors with hearing loss**, the tram has borrowable assistive-listening devices. To arrange an assistive-listening device or for support on the observation tower, I would advise contacting the park at least a week before you plan to visit if you plan to take the Shark Valley tram (phone: 305-242-7700 or TDD: 305-242-7740).

Everglades' Facilities

Unlike other parks in the system, with the Everglades, it is important to consider the main visitor centers alongside travel in the park, as four of the five visitor centers lie at the extremities of the park and act as entrances to and points of departure from Everglades NP. The four entrances to Everglades NP are based in Miami Dade County, Monroe County, and Collier County, with three being land entrances in what are more or less the suburbs of Miami, Everglades City, and Homestead, while the other is on the coastline of the Florida Bay.

These visitor centers are usually open throughout the year although visiting times vary according to the season you visit, which often runs from May through November. I would advise you to contact the individual center closest to the area you plan to visit before you arrive to check when they open, especially as some have been damaged in recent extreme weather and so can include what can best be called scratch facilities.

The **Gulf Coast Visitor Center** (815 Oyster Bar Lane, Everglades City, FL 34139, phone: 239-695-3311) is the main entrance to the area of the Everglades NP for the mangrove islands known as Ten Thousand Islands, which stretch down to the eastern side of the Gulf to Florida Bay. At the time of writing, this visitor center was based in a temporary building, as the original one was destroyed by a recent hurricane. The visitor center is also on a campground and has concession food, as well as concessioner water-sports facilities and tours, including a ninety-minute tour of Chokoloskee Bay, Indian Key Pass, and the mangrove islands.

For **visitors with vision loss**, there is a touch table with tactile exhibits, large-print materials if you ask on arrival, and signs with clear type for those with low vision. For **visitors with mobility access needs**, there are a number of accessible parking spaces for large as well as regular-sized automobiles, and there is an elevator to get into the center from the parking lot. Many of the boat tours advertised as going from the nearby Flamingo and Gulf Coast are wheelchair accessible, and these can be checked out from the Gulf Coast Visitor Center. For **visitors with hearing loss** at the Gulf Coast Visitor Center, a number of the educational and information videos shown in the building have closed captioning.

Near the Homestead entrance to the park, less than a mile from the outer limits of the suburbs of Homestead and a little off the Ingraham Highway, is the **Ernest F. Coe Visitor Center** (40001 State Road 9336, Homestead, FL 33034, phone: 305-242-7700). The Ernest F. Coe Visitor Center is a main education center for Everglades NP, is close to the southeastern area of the national park, known as the Southern Glades, and is around one mile from the Royal Palm area as the crow flies.

The Ernest F. Coe Visitor Center has a large parking lot, areas that display locally created artworks, educational museum exhibitions, a small theater for talks and programs, and movies about the park and its human and natural history. The center also advertises information and brochures about the park and its scenery and wildlife, and it has a bookstore that provides not just books but also a few extra general goods and the all-important water, which you'll need in this subtropical climate.

For **visitors with mobility access needs**, the Ernest F. Coe Visitor Center has a number of accessible parking spaces, including spaces for larger automobiles, a largely accessible pathway from the parking lot, a ramp leading from the pathway, and a button-operated door. Nearby, the Royal Palm visitor area and concession bookstore is largely accessible for those with mobility access needs and has a ramp from the road surface to the sidewalk and building. A number of nearby tours and trails are also largely accessible to **visitors with mobility access needs**, including those who use wheelchairs.

For **visitors with vision loss**, the visitor center also has a number of rolling touchable exhibits on wildlife in the park, and spaces such as the bathrooms and theater have signs in Braille. For those wanting the touchable exhibits, I would advise contacting the desk about these pieces before you tour the general exhibition. For **visitors**

with hearing loss, a number of the educational videos shown in the visitor center have closed captions, and there are assistive-listening devices if you are joining up with a ranger-led interpretive program. The number of assistive-listening devices is limited, however, and so cannot be guaranteed when you visit.

Some way farther into the park from the entrance and near channels of water is the **Shark Valley Visitor Center** (36000 SW 8th Street, Miami, FL 33194, phone: 305-221-8776). The visitor center has bathrooms that are largely accessible, nearby walking or rolling trails, a concession store with parks goods, education displays and videos, and written information about the park. There is also a connected concessioner with rentable bikes that can be used on the nearby road for independent tours of the park or tickets for less independent tours via a local tram. Close by, there are also trails, one of which is largely accessible.

For **visitors with vision loss**, the Shark Valley Visitor Center has touchable exhibits in its collection and Braille signage on a number of its facilities, including its bathrooms. For **visitors with mobility access needs**, the center is largely accessible from the outside and from its parking lot, where there are also accessible spaces. There are also borrowable wheelchairs inside the center; however, the wheelchairs are limited in number, and so their availability can't be guaranteed. The nearby concession tram tour is also accessible and has a ramp to mount the tram and ramps—albeit steep—at various stops during the tour.

Perhaps the most distinctive visitor center in what is thought of as the Everglades NP backcountry, the **Flamingo Visitor Center** (1 Flamingo Lodge Highway, Homestead, FL 33034, phone: 239-695-2945) only opens regularly during the winter months through to early spring, after which there are irregular hours and days of opening largely because of high temperatures and weather conditions. Being on the coast, this center is an education and information hub largely for the sea life in the sea portion of the park and is the beginning of a number of rough trails with varying accessibility. It also has a store with basic essentials and park goods and concessioners that hire watercraft to explore the area. There is also an adjoining backcountry campground.

For **visitors with mobility access issues**, there are accessible parking spaces and a ramp onto the waterfront, although you should be cautious when using this. As with the other visitor centers, the center also has borrowable wheelchairs, although there are limited numbers, and their availability can't be guaranteed.

If you need medical assistance in the park or you need permanent medical support, the following are medical centers or places that can be reached or that can provide treatment or support while you visit the Everglades NP. The Everglades NP has one big advantage over many other wilderness-based national parks, in that it has large and impressive cities nearby, with broad health-care centers. In addition, there is the added advantage that a number of these health-care centers are contactable through a single e-mail address: contact.miamidade@flhealth.gov.

These medical centers include:

- **Health District Center** at 1350 NW 14th Street, Miami, FL 33125. Phone: 305-575-3800.

- **West Perrine Health Center** at 18255 Homestead Avenue, Miami, FL 33157. Phone: 305-234-5400.

- **Little Haiti Health Center** at 300 NE 80th Terrace, Miami, FL 33138. Phone: 305-795-2100.

- **Frederica Wilson and Juanita Mann Health Center** at 2520 NW 75th Street, Miami, FL 33147. Phone: 786-336-1300.

- **Florida City Clinic** at 1600 NW 6th Court, Building B, Florida City, FL 33034. Phone: 305-525-3800.

- **Goulds WIC Center** at 10300 SW 216th Street, Goulds, FL 33190. Phone: 786-336-1300.

- **South Miami WIC Center** at 6601 SW 62nd Avenue, Miami, FL 33143. Phone: 786-336-1300.

- **West Dade WIC Center** at 11865 SW 26th Street, Unit J-6, Miami, FL 33175. Phone: 786-336-1300.

- **Homestead WIC Center** at 753 West Palm Drive, Miami, FL 33034. Phone: 786-336-1300.

- **Carol City WIC Center** at 4737 NW 183rd Street, Miami, FL 33055. Phone: 305-324-2400.

- **Jackson Memorial Hospital WIC Center** at 1611 NW 12th Avenue, Park Plaza West Garage, G-101, Miami, FL 33136. Phone: 786-336-1300.

- **Unity Central WIC Center** at 1490 NW 25th Avenue, 2nd Floor, Miami, FL 33125. Phone: 786-336-1300.

- **University WIC Center** at 1607 SW 107th Avenue, 2nd Floor, Miami, FL 33165. Phone: 786-336-1300.

- **Hialeah West WIC Center** at 551 West 51st Place, 3rd Floor, Hialeah, FL 33012. Phone: 786-336-1300.

- **North Miami Beach WIC Center** at 16855 NE 2nd Avenue, Suite 205, North Miami Beach, FL 33162. Phone: 786-336-1300.

- **Naranja Community Health WIC Center** at 13805 SW 264th Street, Naranja, FL 33032. Phone: 786-336-1300.

- **Dr. Rafael A. Peñalver Clinic** at 971 NW 2nd Street, Miami, FL 33128. Phone: 305-324-2400.

Lodges and Campgrounds

As I wrote about the availability of medical centers, the Everglades NP is notably different from many other wilder national parks as it is close to major cities, known for their tourist industries, hotels, highways, and transport. As a consequence, it's possible to have an accessible vacation visiting the park by day and eating and sleeping accessibly and comfortably at night in a city. However, this approach means missing out on so much of the experience of visiting the park and learning about its surroundings.

Camping in the Everglades can be split into two distinctive experiences: front country and backcountry. Front-country campgrounds include the Long Pine Key, which is a little ways away from Royal Palms and a little farther in from the Homestead entrance to the park, and the Flamingo campgrounds (1 Flamingo Lodge Highway, Homestead, FL 33034, phone: 239-695-1095). Each of these campgrounds is close to other facilities, and Flamingo is close by the Flamingo Visitor Center. You'll need to book in advance of traveling, and I would advise contacting the campgrounds at least three months before you plan to travel both to reserve a space and to let them know about your access needs so these can be accommodated best.

Both of these campgrounds are reachable via small and large automobiles and have generally accessible facilities, such as largely accessible bathrooms, water and washing and showering spaces (although this is generally cold water out of the faucet), and close parking spaces for small and large automobiles. Concessioners can also provide sophisticated, glamorous camping where you can rent a clean and serviced tent or trailer-type accommodation, some of which are very large and have their own beds.

These campgrounds, as I write about above, are also close to developed trails and are largely accessible to **visitors with mobility access issues**. The Flamingo Campground also has large outdoor eating spaces for groups and outdoor cooking facilities, a store that is part of the visitor center complex, and an amphitheater for ranger talks and programs. These talks are seasonal, however, and only available in the relatively cooler months when most of the visitors choose to come.

The only backcountry campground is Pearl Bay Chickee, which as you might expect is far away from roads and can only be approached via water—you'll need to travel several miles from all the other visitor centers and roads and park farther into the Everglades before traveling there. For people with access needs, this campsite is not easy to reach and, being backcountry, does not have running water or regular washing facilities or stores nearby. When you are there, you are pretty much there for the night. However, it does have largely good facilities for **visitors with mobility access needs**, such as a basic accessible bathroom and rail to get around if needed. This being said, it would be difficult to access the campground with a wheelchair.

Learning Programs and Tours

As with the rest of Everglades NP and the other national parks featured in this book—and indeed most national parks in the US—the park generally runs most of its education programs seasonally, when the subtropical climate appeals to the visitors most. As with other parks, in times of less extreme weather there is a full range of ranger-led programs generally in the visitor centers, just outside the centers, or in the Flamingo Campsite amphitheater or guided tours of the nearby largely accessible trails, such as the well-known Anhinga Trail.

One particular program worth mentioning in this chapter is the unique Boater Education Program for people who want to use their own or others' vessels in the national park or similar waters while respecting the environment. This program was developed in conjunction with the Eppley Institute for Parks and Public Lands, Florida Bay Stewardship Committee, and South Florida National Parks Trust (https://www.nps.gov/ever/planyourvisit/boater-education-program.htm).

To find out more about the park's programs and to find out about their accessibility, I would advise contacting the park directly before you plan to visit to find the best and most suitable program for your needs (phone: 305-242-7700 or TDD: 305-242-7740). Of course, at the time of writing this book, we are experiencing an unprecedented pandemic, and so the tours will be largely if not wholly curtailed; however, this should improve in the future.

Beyond the official ranger-led tours, there are also a number of concessioner tours on trams, regular and hover boats and canoes, as well as on foot. As these are concessionary tours and programs, I am not going into detail about these in this book, but there is information on the Everglades NP website and the concession websites. However, these tours are licensed and insured as businesses, and Everglades NP goes to great lengths to emphasize it does not "provide any specific recommendations or assess the specific content of these tours through the current review process." For **visitors with hearing loss**, some boat and tram tours have borrowable assisted-listening devices; I would advise you to check with the relevant tour concessioner about these devices when you book your tour.

Featured Online Learning

Among Everglades NP's learning material, perhaps the most interesting are its online "Nature" materials. These feature largely accessible web pages on the animals found in and around the park, backcountry wilderness areas in the park, the marine life found around Florida Bay, climate change and the environment, the exquisite Florida panther, endangered animals and plants around the park, and the dangers of fire to the natural environment of the park.

For schoolchildren studying in the park or at home, there is also the "Wilderness 101" program. Among other issues, this program features more than one million acres in the park known as the Marjory Stoneman Douglas Wilderness, which is a protected wilderness of rare animals and plants on land and in the water. The program includes digital and paper materials and lesson plans and largely accessible documents for **visitors with hearing loss** and **visitors with vision loss,** although some materials are PDFs that may not work too well with a number of screen readers, and there are no captions (https://www.nps.gov/ever/learn/nature/wilderness101.htm).

These materials and lesson plans for different school grades are partly funded by the South Florida National Parks Trust and Peacock Foundation Inc.[5] If you can't or don't want to access these documents online, you can ask for paper versions from the Everglades Education Department (phone: 305-242-7753). For **visitors with hearing loss** and **visitors with sight loss,** you can also request alternative materials.

GETTYSBURG, PENNSYLVANIA

Address: 1195 Baltimore Pike, Gettysburg, PA 17325

Phone: 717-334-1124

Website: https://www.nps.gov/gett/index.htm

Accessibility website: https://www.nps.gov/gett/planyourvisit/accessibility.htm

---

Pennsylvania

Verbal Image

Pennsylvania is one of the original, administrative colonial-era states of the US and as such is known as a commonwealth rather than a state. Founded by the Quaker William Penn as a gift of land from the British king in 1681, the name Pennsylvania is a mixture of Latin and Old English and literally means "the woodland of Penn." North to south Pennsylvania is around 170 miles (a little over 270 kilometers) tall and a little over 280 miles (around 455 kilometers) wide. Its land covers over 44,740 square miles (over 115,880 square kilometers).[1]

As for its human geography, Pennsylvania is known as the Keystone or Quaker State and is a more urban state than many of the others I feature in this book, with a population of more than 12,805,000. Like many of the other states that were defined in the early days of the union, the shape of the borders of Pennsylvania is a classical rectangle. This rectangle is wide and short, with right-angled borders to all its sides apart from its ragged eastern border, which follows the natural lines of its boundary mountain range. Pennsylvania looks as if it is sloping down on the map, from its higher northeastern borders to its lower southwestern edges.

Moving clockwise around the map, to the north Pennsylvania borders the state of New York and Lake Erie; to the east is New Jersey; to its south are Delaware and Maryland; the southwestern right angle of its border is encased by West Virginia; and Ohio is to its western border. Inside the commonwealth, Philadelphia is the largest city in Pennsylvania and ranks as the sixth most populated in the United States. Pittsburgh is the second-largest city, followed by Allentown, Erie, Reading, and Scranton.

The tall and rugged interior of Pennsylvania is least accessible in the winter, and the west, particularly the northwest districts that wrap Lake Erie, can be particularly difficult to get to during heavy snowfalls. The Appalachian mountain range divides the state, as it runs from the northeast of the US on its way down to the southern states, with this range forming the Allegheny Plateau and various river valleys in the commonwealth. Its only saltwater coastline is the 57 miles along the Delaware Estuary, and as such it does not face the Atlantic directly, with its biggest body of water being the freshwater Lake Erie.

Climate and Wildlife

As I wrote above, the northwestern parts of Pennsylvania are less accessible in the winter, as it is colder than the east and is rainier and snowier than its moderate southern regions. Pennsylvania has summer day temperatures around 75 F (almost 24 C) to 95 F (around

35 C), while nights are around 55 F (almost 13 C) to 70 F (around 21 C). Winter highs average around 33 F (less than 1 C) to 45 F (over 7 C), while its low temperatures are around 19 F (more than –7 C) to around 30 F (more than 1 C). July is the peak of summer in Pennsylvania, and during this peak month, its temperatures can occasionally touch around 100 F (almost 38 C), while January is by far the coldest month, when its temperatures can go below 0 F (almost –18 C).[2]

Pennsylvania can get cyclones, severe snowstorms, and tornadoes, and the commonwealth has an average annual snowfall over 100 inches (around 2,540 millimeters) and an average rainfall around 42 inches (almost 1,070 millimeters). Pennsylvania also averages around 180 days of sunshine during the year, although cloudy skies are common in the state throughout the year. Phoenixville recorded Pennsylvania's highest temperature of around 111 F (almost 44 C) in July 1936, while Smethport recorded the lowest temperature of around –42 F (more than –41 C) in January 1904.

Pennsylvania's wildlife, plants, and trees reflect its diverse, complex geography. The commonwealth is particularly known for beavers in its rivers, bobcats in its highlands, chipmunks, Appalachian cottontails, elk, numerous species of bats, opossum, black bears, coyotes, red fox, porcupine, the rare red squirrel, river otters, bald eagles, and wild turkeys. In its abundant forests, you can find beautifully named sugar maples, red cedar, green ash, eastern hemlock, sumac, eastern white pine, black ash, sweet birch, and flowering dogwood. As for its plants and bushes, Pennsylvania is known for speckled and smooth alders, cranberry bushes, wild columbine, monarda, and the elegant blue lobelia.

Gettysburg National Military Park

Verbal Image

Created on the famous piece of land that was fought over in July 1863, Gettysburg National Military Park[3] (Gettysburg NP) was founded to commemorate the Civil War's Battle of Gettysburg, otherwise called the "High Water Mark of the Rebellion." This battle led to an unforgettable victory for the Union troops and subsequently became the scene of Abraham Lincoln's "Gettysburg Address." The Battle of Gettysburg has since been thought of as a turning point in the Civil War in the cultural memory of the US.

Gettysburg NP is very different from other parks in this book, as its purpose is not to preserve wilderness or nature, although when you get to the park, you'll notice that it has this evergreen nature too. Gettysburg is preserved for its historical significance to the shape and story of the US and its international significance for US governance.

The origins of the park came not long after the battle in 1864, when Gettysburg Battlefield Memorial Association was formed to remember the fallen soldiers. After the foundation of the association and motivated by the aim of building a memorial to the Union and its soldiers, in 1895 the federal government passed a bill legally mandating the Gettysburg National Military Park. During this period, Civil War veterans became part of its administration and oversaw its early restoration process, which continued until, in 1933, the National Parks Service took over the memorial, and it officially became a national park.

Gettysburg NP is comfortably over six thousand acres and made up of a tall, thin, geometrical head on a long neck with straight angular boundaries. Unlike other parks in this book, Gettysburg is also close to large urban areas and transport links and does not have much of what can be described as wilderness within its boundaries. Certainly, it is not the kind of wilderness that you will find in the other parks in this book.

Gettysburg NP is in Adams County, and most of the park is just off the Baltimore Pike. Getting to Gettysburg NP is relatively easy, as the park is not far from major cities. For instance, the park is generally less than forty miles or around forty-five minutes' drive from Harrisburg, the capital of Pennsylvania, and less than eighty miles and around an hour-and-a-half drive from Washington, DC.

A little farther afield, Philadelphia is just over two-and-a-quarter hours and a little less than 150 miles from the park; Pittsburgh is just under 185 miles and just over three-and-a-quarter hours' drive.

Getting Around Gettysburg

As with other parks in this book, Gettysburg NP relies strongly on shuttle buses, as driving is largely restricted on its main campus. However, given the nature of the park, these shuttle buses are run in a different way and are linked to famous historical sites both in the park and those not far outside it. For instance, not far off from the park is President Eisenhower's house and farm, which can be visited via shuttle bus from Gettysburg NP Museum and Visitor Center in around seven minutes.

There are also two-hour-long tours of Gettysburg Battlefield, which in good weather take place on an open double-decker bus or, in the rain, snow, or cold, take place on a regular, covered single-decker bus. Although the tour is not run by the park itself, the tour employs a National Parks Service–approved guide. For those wanting to follow this tour, visitors are asked to board up to five minutes before it starts.

The open bus tour begins at the Museum and Visitor Center and drives up to the Eisenhower farm and other historical sites on its route. As this is a concession tour, I am not going to cover this more; however, it is important to note that for **visitors with mobility access issues**, provisions can be made for them to use their automobiles around the park if they cannot board the bus.

There are also many opportunities for walking around Gettysburg NP via walking tours, such as the independent Cemetery Ridge Trail Walking Tour and the National Cemetery Walking Tour guided by a predesigned trail. Visitors pick up guides of the National Cemetery Walking Tour from the park information desk and for the Cemetery Ridge Trail from the park bookstore (more about these places below). In addition to the guidebook tours, there are also regular trails around Big Round Top and Little Round Top,

Devil's Den, and Pickett's Charge, and it is important to check with the visitor center about these too.

For **visitors with mobility access needs**, the park estimates that half of the Cemetery Ridge Trail is largely accessible as you move over its paved trails, as the land is generally flat. The National Cemetery can also be toured, although it is notable that rangers at the visitor center's information desk can give permission to drive the road around the cemetery via automobile if you are a **visitor with severe mobility access needs**. I would advise you to contact the park before you visit to ask about these permissions (phone: 717-334-1124). When you get past the road, the cemetery is mainly lawned and, although relatively flat, is less accessible; in addition, all visitors at all times should remember to be silent and respectful of the fallen soldiers in the cemetery.

Visitors are also allowed to cycle ride certain parts of the park, and if visitors choose to ride, they should also find it relatively accessible. However, visitors also need to note that there are general restrictions that apply to all the public roads in the area around Adams County. For example, the park warns visitors that its roads get a lot of traffic, particularly during tourist seasons, and so you will need to be cautious if you bring a bicycle.

Visitors also need to be aware that you can only ride on official roads and avenues, as riding in the National Cemetery or the National Cemetery Annex or on trails and across fields in the parkland is banned. Although you can walk your bikes over trails and within the cemetery, like walkers, you'll need to show respect once you're inside its boundary. For visitors wanting to park their bicycles in the park, there are racks that are located at both entrances and in one of the parking lots of the Museum and Visitor Center.

Motorized e-bikes are also generally allowed in Gettysburg NP in all the areas that regular bicycles can go and are subject to the same regulations. However, it seems to be best to check with the park before bringing these bikes, as there are some further complications related to these vehicles. These regulations are on different pages on the park's website (https://www.nps.gov/gett/learn/news/electric-bicycles.htm).

For those on bicycles or automobiles, there are more than twenty-five miles of largely accessible paved roads, and highways 15, 116, 134, and 30 continue all or partway through the park. For **visitors with mobility access needs**, rangers at the visitor center's information desk can give permission to drive the road around the cemetery via automobile. However, as before, I'd advise checking with the park before visiting to see if you qualify for this permission. As the park told me, "[If] you go back to the early years of the battlefield park, many of the roads/park avenues were built with the intention that they would provide access to mobility impaired veterans, who were then predominantly in their late 70s [and] early 80s."

If you are given permission to ride in an automobile, you will also be able to stop at historically important sites and exhibits, which are flagged by signs and other instructions on paths along the tour route. Visitors should note that many of these stops are in grassy areas and less accessible than the asphalt area and that the auto tour brochure can tell you the story of a number of stops and gives information about the ground they are on. In addition, rangers are based around the parkland and can give visitors more information and discuss the battle at important sites on the battlefield and along the route.

Gettysburg's Facilities

Gettysburg NP has the advantage in that it has a number of facilities and important visitable sites concentrated into such a small area. However, wherever visitors want to get to in the park, they will mostly start their trip at the Gettysburg Foundation's **Gettysburg National Military Park Museum and Visitor Center** (1195 Baltimore Pike, Gettysburg, PA 17325, phone: 717-334-2436). "In 2008 the new Museum and Visitor Center opened, which was the first time the NPS at Gettysburg had a museum [or] visitor center facility that was truly designed with accessibility in mind." This Museum and Visitor Center is an extensive information and education complex, with ticket booking services, a place to buy hot food and drink, a bookstore, and national park membership booking. The museum is large and has an extensive collection of Civil War objects and artworks. The visitor center is also the hub and focal point for the shuttle and tour buses around and in and out of the park, and there is a parking lot nearby. In addition, there is also a National Parks Service Information Desk with permanent rangers within the visitor center to provide spoken information and grant permissions.

The Gettysburg NP advertises two highlights in this visitor center. The first highlight is the film, *A New Birth of Freedom*, on the Civil War and Battle of Gettysburg. This film is narrated by Morgan Freeman and shown throughout the day, although the frequency of shows changes throughout the year. The second highlight is the roughly forty-foot-tall cyclorama painting that was created by the artist Paul Philippoteaux and other members of his studio over the course of a year and that depicts different scenes from the Civil War.

Throughout the center and museum, there are also auditoria for presentations, exhibitions, lectures, and films, and visitors can also hire a licensed and self-employed battlefield guide in the center to show them the best historical sites in the park. These private tours last two hours, as the bus tours do, and these guides can travel in private automobiles with **visitors with access needs**.

For **visitors with sight loss**, the center and museum have touchable exhibits and artifacts. The center is also largely accessible for **visitors with mobility access needs,** with largely accessible restrooms, a film auditorium, and a cyclorama auditorium. The center also has free borrowable wheelchairs that can be asked for at the National Parks Service Information Desk, although numbers of these chairs are limited so their availability cannot be guaranteed.

For **visitors with hearing loss**, the auditorium and cyclorama have borrowable assisted-listening devices. You can ask about these devices at the ticket counter when you get your tickets, although I would strongly advise that you contact the center before you visit, to make sure these devices can be made available.

The David Wills House was the home of the attorney of the same name and the house in which President Abraham Lincoln finished writing his Gettysburg Address. This house is also a museum with galleries and rooms that have been made to look as they did in 1863, including the bedroom President Lincoln stayed in when he composed his life-changing speech.

For **visitors with mobility access needs**, the house has largely accessible restrooms and an elevator to generally less accessible parts of the building. However, I'd advise that you check with the center if you are in a wheelchair for dimensions of the bathroom and elevator doors. For **visitors with hearing loss**, the house has borrowable assisted-listening devices that you can request at the house's information desk.

The **Eisenhower National Historic Site** was the former president's weekend home and farm, is near Gettysburg Battlefield, and is largely preserved from the time he stayed there. For **visitors with mobility access needs**, the park can provide someone to assist with getting to the first floor. However, it should be borne in mind that this is a historical house, and since the upper floors are up stairs, the building can be less accessible.

For visitors who cannot reach the upper floors and who have sight, the house has a photo book of the rooms and a number of the objects on the second floor. There are also free borrowable wheelchairs, although their numbers are limited and not guaranteed. For **visitors with hearing loss**, there are written descriptions of the house tour that can substitute for a spoken tour. Visitors can ask the ranger in attendance at the house or other staff members or volunteers for these descriptions. Similarly, **visitors with sight loss** can also ask for a large-print guide for the same tour.

As I have written above, the one great advantage of Gettysburg NP is that it is near major cities and developed towns, and so you are never too far from medical help. For those needing medical assistance in the park or permanent medical support when traveling, the following are medical centers: **WellSpan Washington St. Health Center** (450 South Washington Street, phone: 717-338-3290) and **WellSpan Gettysburg Hospital** (147 Gettys Street, phone: 717-334-2121). The rest can be found in nearby towns and are numerous.

Lodges and Campgrounds

Visitors who want to lodge or camp have more choice outside the park than within it. However, as these outside places are commercial hotels, lodges, and campgrounds, I will not be describing them here. For those visitors who want to stay in the park, it offers a historic site called the Bushman House as a year-round place to stay; it is located within the boundaries of Gettysburg National Military Park and stood during the Battle of Gettysburg.

Bushman House is near the town of Gettysburg and has three bedrooms; shared bathrooms; a modern kitchen with facilities for cooking, storing food, and eating; as well as a dining room and sitting room. This makes it an option for people wanting to share with a group they know well. Visitors can book the house on the Recreation.gov website and will have to sign a short-term lease with the National Parks Service. This is a popular place to stay, so I would advise you to contact the park or look into booking several months in advance, if possible, and look at the facilities online at least six months in advance.

For those who want to camp in the park, the only option is the McMillan Woods Youth Campground. However, this campground is reserved as space for organizations such as the Scouts and other official groups of young people, such as classes and church groups. In the campground, only one adult is allowed to stay with each group for every ten youths, and these individuals are usually restricted to scoutmasters or youth counselors, not lone parents or groups of families alone.

Based on West Confederate Avenue within the park boundaries, the campground has basic bathrooms, water, and trash facilities, and for **visitors with mobility access issues**, there is only a single accessible bathroom. The park also has strict rules, and campers are expected to be silent and not walk around the park between 10 p.m. to 6 a.m.; there are no outside lighted areas, alcohol is not allowed, and recreational vehicles and buses are banned from the campground. The campground is open from spring through early fall. I would strongly advise booking several months in advance (phone: 717-334-1124, website: https://www .recreation.gov).

Learning Programs and Tours

The park makes the following recommendations for **visitors with access needs**: "Experience the orientation and cyclorama programs, and then see the battlefield. This can be done in so many different ways that any individual, regardless of their mobility or age, can have a meaningful experience. We have bus tours, personally guided tours in your own vehicle, and hikes, walks, and static programs that cater to the diverse array of visitors we get."

As I wrote above, there are a number of independent and ticketed educational opportunities in the visitor centers, including the park film, the extensive cyclorama, and the museum exhibits themselves. Out in the park, there are also battlefield and historical tours for groups, which are given by licensed guides, and these include a number of the historic places listed above and also a number of the outdoor exhibits that are around the park. These exhibits include the park's Abraham Lincoln bust in the National Cemetery, Eisenhower's farm, Rupp House History Center, and George Spangler Farm and Field Hospital, among others.

In addition to independent and self-guided tours, Gettysburg NP also has education programs and packaged tours run by the park or self-employed and licensed guides. In addition, park rangers and guest historians give talks for free in the park that last around one hour. These talks and programs largely chart the history and geography of the Battle of Gettysburg and the political outcomes of the battle and the Civil War.

For adults, the park also runs special programs often with external organizations for groups who want to know more about the park. "We've established a partnership with Project Odyssey, a subgroup of the Wounded Warrior Project. As part of the program, we provide meaningful and in-depth programming aimed at participants in the Wounded Warrior Project. They come to us with a variety of challenges from mobility issues to more emotional/psychological struggles. It's one of the more rewarding things we do."

Featured Online Learning

Although the park does not have its own app, as some of the larger parks do, it is part of the general app put out by the National Parks Service and distributes information through it: "Our park brochure and 'unigrid' is available in an app known as UniD, as a fully functional audio description. We also feature a virtual tour on our park website, which is mobile friendly."

In common with other parks featured in this book, Gettysburg NP offers distance-learning programs, although these are largely targeted at school classes. For instance, at the time of writing, the park offered Virtual Field Trip Ranger Programs. Prior to the tour, students get to choose from ten of its focused questions and use them to investigate the battle, the park, and the history of the US during and after the Civil War.

The tour consists of a film introducing the park to the class, a set of scanned or replicated documents from the time of the Battle of Gettysburg and the Civil War, and a talk with a question-and-answer session by a ranger from the park. The tour can be personalized for each age, school, grade, and class, and it is adaptable. You should contact the park's education center for more information, and to organize and personalize a tour, write to the park via its messaging link on its Contact Us web page. However, I would advise you to contact the park at least three months before you want to arrange your tour, as they are popular, and the availability of rangers cannot be guaranteed.[4]

Specialized Access

For **visitors with hearing loss**, Gettysburg NP can contract ASL signers to accompany tours of the park if given enough notice, and there is no cost for this support in addition to the normal tour or ticket costs. I would advise contacting the park at least two months in advance, as it takes time to make sure a signer is available. For **visitors with mobility access needs**, the park also has borrowable wheelchairs in the visitor center and will modify their operations to support visitors on tours and around the visitor centers and the museum. For **visitors with sight loss**, the park can also arrange Braille versions of park brochures and provide audio-described tour and learning materials. Again, I would advise contacting the park at least one month before you plan to visit to order these materials, which are free to arrange (phone: 717-334-1124).

GRAND CANYON, ARIZONA

Address: PO Box 129, Grand Canyon, AZ 86023
Phone: 928-638-7888
E-mail: grca_information@nps.gov
Website: www.nps.gov/grca

Arizona

Verbal Image

Arizona is a largely desert and wilderness state with a population of more than 6,930,000. However, this is not the wilderness of the Everglades nor the wilderness of Maine or Alaska. This is a wilderness of dry and cavernous regions and a desert of jagged rocks and extreme heat. As it lies on the map, Arizona is a little less than 350 miles (almost 550 kilometers) wide and a little under 400 miles (almost 640 kilometers) tall and has an area of a little under 115,000 square miles (a little over 295,000 square kilometers). To underline how dry this state is, of this area, the dry land takes up over 113,500 square miles (almost 294,00 square kilometers).[1]

The shape of Arizona is largely rectangular with die-straight north and east borders forming an almost solid right angle. Along its other sides, it has an uneven yet still geometric line on its southern border where it meets Mexico and a rough and jagged line to its natural western boundary line.

The main river, deserts, and mountains of Arizona also lie on its borders, which clockwise touch New Mexico to the east; the Mexican states of Sonora and Baja California Norte to the south; to the west, California and Nevada; and Utah to the north. The northeastern, almost right-angled tip of Arizona also touches Colorado, and it is from here that the largest water source, the Colorado River, flows. This river is important to Arizona, as it brings glacial and mountain waters from high in the Rocky Mountain range, forms part of the border with Nevada and all of the border with California, and then drops down into Mexico and into the sea.

For a largely desert state, Arizona is surprisingly high above sea level, with an average height around 1,250 meters, although that might be due to the Grand Canyon itself; its highest mountain is the snow-covered Humphrey's Peak at over 3,800 meters high, whereas the lowest point is a mere 22 meters, which is the lowest point of the Colorado River. Beyond its desert climate, its mountains, and its famous canyons, Arizona is also known for its plateaus and forests.

Culturally, and perhaps because living in its desert areas is difficult, most of Arizona's population is centered in its large cities of Phoenix, with a population of over 1,600,000; Tucson, with more than 540,000; Mesa, with almost 500,000; and Chandler and Scottsdale, each with more than 250,000 people. Being dry, however, it is difficult to farm, and so its largest produce off the land is livestock, most importantly cattle farming.

Climate and Wildlife

In keeping with its place on the US–Mexican border and makeup largely of desert, it is perhaps unsurprising that Arizona averages more than 190 clear days of sunshine a year. Its average temperature is above 60 F (more than 15 C), with an average summer temperature over 78 F (over 25 C) and an average winter temperature over 43 F (6 C). However, like its average height, these temperatures poorly reflect the extreme hot and cold in the state, as the desert cools dramatically at night with, of course, its high peaks being much cooler than its deserts during the day.[2]

To illustrate these extremes of temperature, Arizona's record highest temperature was around a shockingly high 128 F (more than 53 C) at Lake Havasu City in June 1994, while its record low temperature was an astonishingly low −40 F (−40 C) in January 1971 at Hawley Lake. Arizona's average annual rain- and snowfall is equally deceptive, with an annual rainfall a little over 13.5 inches (almost 350 millimeters) and snow falling around 0.3 days a year and less than 0.5 inches (less than 1 centimeter) in depth. Of course, some of its mountains have some snow most of the year.

Similarly, given its extremes of hot and cold, desert and mountain, Arizona has extremely interesting wildlife, trees, and plant life. Its animals include the unique and rare tassel-eared Kaibab squirrel, bears, the rattlesnake (the iconic animal of the desert), bighorn sheep, coyotes, and—the inspiration for the cartoon—the roadrunner. Farther into the woodland and tundra, you will also find mule deer, elks, the fascinatingly titled Gila monsters, horned toads, jackrabbits, jaguars, mountain lions, prairie dogs, and wild turkeys.

The state's plants are similarly variable, with the desert being ruled by the legally protected cacti; then there are the beautifully named chollas, desert grass, fluted saguaros, mesquites, ocotillo bush, organ pipes, prickly pears, and yucca. As for its trees, you can also find aspens, Douglas firs, junipers, maples, oaks, the unusual Palo Verde trees, pines, pinyons, the wonderfully designated ponderosa trees, spruce, and walnut.

Grand Canyon National Park

Verbal Image

I would guess only a few places in the world can be called a natural world landmark, and the Grand Canyon National Park[3] (Grand Canyon NP) can truly be called one. In the US, although the Rockies and Denali are magnificent, they do not rival the Himalayas for height or scope; although the Everglades are truly beautiful and unique, the tropical forests and swamps of the Amazon basin and the corals of the Great Barrier Reef are larger and wilder and have more endangered species. However, although not the deepest, at around 417,000,000,000 cubic meters, the Grand Canyon is truly the vastest and largest canyon by volume in the world. This size and its natural uniqueness have contributed to its listing as a UNESCO World Heritage Site:

> Carved out by the Colorado River, the Grand Canyon (nearly 1,500 m deep) is the most spectacular gorge in the world. Located in the state of Arizona, it cuts across the Grand Canyon National Park. Its horizontal strata retrace the geological history of the past 2 billion years. There are also prehistoric traces of human adaptation to a particularly harsh environment.[4]

Formed from tectonically shifting rocks and the erosion that defines it shape, much of the area of the Grand Canyon legally became a government-mandated reserve in 1893 and a national park in 1919. The park is unusual as its entire area is devoted to this single natural geological feature; its fossils, rock strata, wildlife, and plant life; and the thousands of years of human history from the Ice Age until now. As a consequence, the shape of the park is a natural long, thin shape, like a more than 275-mile-long snake passing diagonally from the central north of Arizona to its northwestern border with Nevada. This is a snake that is also a mile or two shy of twenty miles wide at its broadest point.

The canyon was carved out of layers of sedimentary rock over a period of up to six million years from the fast-flowing glacial and Rocky Mountain rainwaters of the Colorado River—although the precise date at which it was first formed is as yet unknown. This made it a seldom-explored and seldom-disturbed wilderness throughout its natural history. The canyon itself is around one mile deep at its lowest point, with the national park itself taking up an area a shade over 1,900 square miles on a map.

The Grand Canyon's volume is so great that it seems to have different climates at different heights of the canyon, with the air temperature varying around five and a half degrees for every one thousand feet you travel up or down. Because of this vast depth and volume, the park itself is divided into three distinct areas—the Colorado River Valley, the North Rim, and the South Rim—although gmost land visits to the canyon stay on the two rims. The North Rim is the highest of the two rims, and its most popular point to visit is the Kaibab Plateau, which has spectacular ponderosa pines and aspens. On the lower South Rim, the most popular place to visit is Mather, which also has ponderosa pines, but also has mixed wooded areas with pinyon and juniper trees.

Although the Grand Canyon averages around 5,900,000 visitors a year, given its vast, gaping chasm and astonishing length, it is of course not possible to drive directly through the Grand Canyon NP between the North Rim and the South Rim. Consequently, unless you choose to trek through or fly over the Colorado River Valley, you often have to choose to travel to its North or South Rim alone in a single visit. This choice also largely determines the town you set out from to reach the national park.

The closest town to the South Rim is Flagstaff at around eighty miles or a little over an hour-and-a-half drive, with the North Rim being around 210 miles, or more than four hours' drive away. By contrast, from Nevada, Las Vegas is relatively speaking close to both rims, and is around 265 miles or over four and a half hours' drive from the North Rim and around 275 miles, or over five hours' drive, from the South Rim. Phoenix, by contrast, is around 350 miles away, or much over six hours' drive, from the South Rim and around 230 miles, or a little under five hours' drive, from the North Rim.

Getting Around Grand Canyon

In common with other parks I've featured in this book, the Grand Canyon has an established shuttle bus service for visitors. But it is on the South Rim, where most visitors come to take in the views or to have a staging post for the internal Colorado River Valley— although when you're planning your visit you should note that the shuttle does not make it to Desert View Road. Operated by the Grand Canyon NP itself, the South Rim shuttles operate four routes in spring, summer, and fall, connecting the visitor center with various lodges, campgrounds, and park attractions. These routes are the Hermit Road (Red) Route, the Kaibab Rim (Orange) Route, the Tusayan Route/Park & Ride, and the Village (Blue) Route.

Generally speaking, the shuttle buses run every fifteen to thirty minutes, although, during winter 2021, the park only had two shuttle routes. There are a number of bus stops around the South Rim, often where it's thought the best views are, and tickets are not needed.

In Grand Canyon NP, there are also special buses for trekkers, called the Hikers' Express Shuttles, from one of its lodges to the South Kaibab Trailhead. These buses run less frequently and may not work all year round or at least they may run less often. I would advise you to check with the national park about the availability of the buses not long before you visit the park. In addition, there is a commercial bus service that carries visitors from the North Rim to the South Rim and vice versa. I am not going to comment further on this service, as it is a commercial service.

For **visitors with mobility access needs**, the shuttle buses are largely accessible, with broad exit steps close to the sidewalk, ramps for those who need them, and spaces to carry visitors in wheelchairs.[5] However, it is important to note that most motorized mobility scooters will not fit on the buses (https://www.nps.gov/grca/plan yourvisit/shuttle-buses.htm).

The Grand Canyon has a number of walking trails along both rims and into the Colorado River Valley itself. These trails vary from pathways that are rough and difficult to travel for walkers with the best balance to those that are shorter but much more manageable and so more accessible. These trails often start or have entry and exit points by visitor centers, campgrounds, and parking lots—see below about visitor centers and campsites for more details—and can be reached by frequent shuttles traveling around the park.

An example of a partly accessible trail is the Rim Trail, which traverses part of the South Rim and takes in the Grand Canyon Village, and from which you can reach its main visitor center or campground. By contrast, on the North Rim, there is a less accessible trail called the North Kaibab Trail that joins up with the main campground on the rim and meanders down into the Colorado River Valley. As with all these trails, I would check very carefully when planning your visit, and there is more detailed information about most trails on the park's website (www.nps.gov/grca).

Unusually for somewhere inside a national park, the Grand Canyon Village has its own railway. Called the Grand Canyon Railway, the line starts in Williams, Arizona, but only travels once or at most twice a day in the tourist season. The view from its railroad cars is particularly special; however, there is variable accessibility on these trains, especially for **visitors with mobility access needs**. I will not go into this route further in this book as it is a commercial line.

Similar to other national parks, the Grand Canyon NP encourages its visitors to take shuttle buses into the park and preferably walk around after they've arrived, although the park does not ban all automobiles as some others do. On the North Rim, as there is no shuttle bus, the only reliable land way to arrive is via automobile, especially for those who plan to camp in the park and who need to bring equipment. However, generally speaking, you will pay a larger entrance fee when you arrive by automobile than if you come using other forms of transport. There are also issues with road access at different times of the year, depending on weather and environmental conditions.

The Grand Canyon NP, however, still recommends using the shuttle buses to travel around the South Rim even if you arrive in an automobile, as you can park on the outskirts of the park or Grand Canyon Village. Importantly, if you take the local shuttle, it's generally free, so you'll save on your gas and also be able to take in the surrounding scenery as you travel. There are also small parking lots en route to the park but no parking at all at sightseeing points, meaning that, generally speaking, you have a better chance of stopping at these sites if you ride the bus. For those taking the shuttle bus, there are various stops where you can hop on and off along the South Rim.

This said, **visitors with mobility access needs** that are severe or the supporters of these visitors can apply for the Grand Canyon NP's Scenic Drive Accessibility Permit. You can ask about this permit when you first arrive at the park at the entrance or visitor centers if you have a disability badge on your automobile, and once granted, the permit allows you onto roads and into parking spaces infrequently open to the public. For more information and to find out about the terms of this permit, I'd advise you to call the park before you visit (phone: 928-638-7888).

Grand Canyon's Facilities

Despite its size, Grand Canyon has few visitor centers; however, those that it has are mostly large and comprehensive complexes, often with concession or park facilities and spaces that act as public transport hubs or are close to the campgrounds. In other words, Grand Canyon NP thinks about the integrated infrastructure of its park, and you can get to and around what is an arid wilderness relatively easily. As always, it should be born in mind that these visitor centers may have different times in different seasons and that these times can be irregular, as they often cope with extreme weather events and natural disasters. As a consequence, I'd advise you to check with the park or look at its website just before you visit, to make sure of what's available at that time.

More or less on the edge of Grand Canyon Village and not far off Highway 64 is **Grand Canyon Visitor Center**, which it can be said is the main hub for information on the park and its activities. It is also a main center for education and learning in the South Rim area, is a major starting point for walking or bicycling trails, and is close to the South Rim's biggest parking lots and public transport stop-off points. Highlights of education within the visitor center that are advertised by the park include the theater, where you can go to talks about natural and human history; the park's video, *Watch Grand Canyon: A Journey of Wonder*, which runs every half hour; and a multimedia relief map named Science On a Sphere.

The outer-village complex surrounding the visitor center also has concessioner stores and services including banking, food and drink outlets, bicycle and other transport hire, and commercial bus stops. Importantly, it is also the shuttle bus staging post for much of the national park and all of the South Rim, and you can park your automobile in one of its four large and nearby parking lots and take the shuttle to all the sightseeing spots in and around the South Rim. The visitor center is also visitable on foot from Mather Point, which has one of the main sightseeing points in the park.

For **visitors with access needs**, you can ask resident park rangers about facilities in the center or the park in general and about providing access facilities. For **visitors with sight loss**, the Science On a Sphere relief map linked to touchable exhibition pieces and Braille labels, and away from the visitor center, a local bank in and a lodge near the complex have ATMs with Brailled information and headphone adapters. In addition, a nearby concessioner rents tandem bicycles for people who ride with sighted guides. For **visitors with hearing loss**, the Science On a Sphere video has open captioning, as do a number of the center's educational videos, and you can ask for borrowable assistive-listening devices during lectures and talks in the center.

Visitors with mobility access needs have largely accessible views of the Colorado River Valley and Phantom Ranch on viewing platforms near the visitor center, and there is a relatively smooth path to these platforms—this includes access for visitors using wheelchairs. In the same complex as the visitor center, concessioners rent wheelchairs for use around the South Rim.

In Grand Canyon Village itself, **Verkamp's Visitor Center** and cultural site has exhibits on the history of the modern human communities who live and work in the park. This visitor center is relatively small and based on a one-hundred-year-old store and family home, with a concession store with park goods. In the center, there are resident park rangers for information and to provide help if you need it, and outside the old building, there is access to a number of walking trails around. As this is a historical building, I'm afraid the access can be variable; however, **visitors with vision loss** can find this an interesting multisensory experience with authentic tactile and olfactory experiences of an old village building.

On the edge of town, in what is termed Grand Canyon Village's Historical District, you can also visit **Kolb Studio**, which in decades past was a photography studio and family home and is now recreated as such for contemporary visitors. This center has exhibitions of historical, photographic, and fine art pieces and displays and written material on Emery and Ellsworth Kolb, who chronicled the Grand Canyon through photographs and movies. Examples of the center's displays at the time of writing include the Grand Canyon Celebration of Art. The center is also just off an established walking trail in Grand Canyon Village that can be followed to a number of viewing points.

Not too far from Grand Canyon Visitor Center and Grand Canyon Village and also based in an old-fashioned building is **Yavapai Geology Museum and Observation Station** on Yavapai Point. This center is on the Kaibab Rim Shuttle bus route, and there are viewpoints here for watching sunsets over the Colorado River Valley and the North Rim. The museum showcases the geological history of the canyon through permanent and temporary exhibits and has a concession store and park goods. You can also use the area around the museum as a staging point to walk trails, including those for the spectacular and infamous Mather Point.

On the South Rim, away from Grand Canyon Village and often not far from Highway 64, there are other specialist visitor and information centers. For instance, **Backcountry Information Center** is where the Hikers' Bus departs. Near Navajo Point is the **Desert View Visitor Center**, which has a museum and American Indian arts, most notably by the Hopi Artist Fred Kabotie. From this center you can also take a ranger-guided tour to the nearby **Tusayan Ruin and Museum**, which has additional ancient American Indian artifacts.

The North Rim has its own North Rim Visitor Center, which also features education exhibitions, information, resident park rangers for information and support, and ranger and specialist talks on the patio of its nearby lodge. The complex around the visitor center also has a saloon and the North Rim Country Store run by Grand Canyon Conservancy, a not-for-profit organization that has been running fundraisers to help preserve the park since 1932.

For **visitors with mobility access needs**, the visitor center's nearby saloon and connected store has partly accessible ATMs at wheelchair height. The visitor center itself has a small number of borrowable wheelchairs. However, as there are not many, their availability cannot be guaranteed.

For those visitors who need medical assistance in the park or who need permanent medical support, the following are medical centers that can be reached or that can provide remote treatment:

- **South Rim Medical Services** in Grand Canyon Village. Phone: 928-638-2551.

- **North Rim Medical Services** on the North Rim, only for emergency medical services by park rangers in the area. Phone: 911.

- **North Country Healthcare—Grand Canyon** at 1 Clinic Road, Grand Canyon Village, AZ 86023. Phone: 928-638-2551.

Lodges and Campgrounds

There are two main campgrounds in Grand Canyon NP, one on the South Rim and the other on the North Rim.

On the South Rim, not far by foot or bus from Grand Canyon Village and close by the Grand Canyon NP Headquarters, is **Mather Campground**. This is the largest campground in the park, is accessible from the shuttle bus from the main visitor center, and has hiking and biking trails close by. It is comfortable and very well resourced, having flushable toilets, picnic tables, barbeques, drinking water facilities, accessible flat and hard campsites and parking, trash collection, utility sinks for washing in, coin-operated showers, security lights, and spaces to wash clothes.

Part of the campground is also a trailer village for visitors with RVs, and this village has hookups and spaces for larger RVs and there is space on-site for horse camping. In addition, there is also a ranger station and areas for wildlife viewing, biking, and horseback riding. There is also a dump station at the nearby camper services on the ground.

The Mather Campground is largely accessible for **visitors with mobility access issues**, although the facilities are rustic and the tent camping has no electricity. The campground itself is, despite being high up on the rim, generally accessible, and you can usually get to its campfire rings, cooking grates, picnic tables, and eating areas easily, and it also allows parking near tents.

The park's **North Rim Campground** is similarly accessible, although it is relatively smaller with not quite as many facilities, is similarly not electric for tent users, and is also rustic and less populated. The North Rim Campground is again more than one thousand feet higher than Mather on the South Rim and can be very hot, can have snow, and can have all the weather in between at different times of the year. As with Mather, the campground has dump stations, picnic tables, campfire rings, cooking grills, outlets for drinking water, coin-operated showers, and a laundry. The North Rim Campground also has a nearby lodge, which at the time of writing had food to take out. There is also a concession store near the campground entrance.

Learning Programs and Tours

The Grand Canyon NP has interactive and multisensory exhibits in all its visitor centers and museums, although a number of these museums are in historical buildings and can't be adapted, as its visitor centers are, to have theater-based educational talks and shows. For instance, on the South Rim, the Grand Canyon Visitor Center runs a twenty-minute film, *Grand Canyon: A Journey of Wonder*, in its theater. Alternatively, the Desert View Cultural Center runs American Indian cultural demonstrations nearby and tours of a former Puebloan village a few miles from the visitor center.

In addition, the Grand Canyon NP runs ranger programs in visitor centers, in lodges, and on trails on topics such as the history of the canyon's geology, its human history and archaeology, and practical programs such as hiking and photography. These programs run according to the seasons, weather conditions depending, with its rolling program available online (https://www.nps.gov/grca/planyourvisit/ranger-program.htm). In addition, the not-for-profit Grand Canyon Conservancy also runs a Field Institute, which organizes daylong and overnight tours throughout the park that include trekking, camping, and raft-riding stretches of the Colorado River. These rafting programs and expeditions can last for several days and up to three weeks.

For **visitors with hearing loss**, the park organizes ASL interpretation for park ranger programs. As these signers are contracted, the park asks that you provide at least three weeks' advance notice before your visit; however, I would advise you to contact the park at least one month in advance and explain your access needs to be sure (phone: 928-638-7888, e-mail: grca_information@nps.gov).

For visitors with mobility access needs, a number of the ranger-led programs are said to be largely accessible, including to those in wheelchairs.

Featured Online Learning

For visitors who cannot make it to the park or visitors who want to learn about the park before traveling there, the Grand Canyon NP has a free, bookable distance-learning program that is largely accessible to **visitors with access needs**. Through these programs, you can learn in your own time or interact with tutors, and you can organize groups through schools, senior centers, and adult learning institutions. At the time of writing, the programs the park offered ran formally from Tuesday through Thursday and included lesson plans and materials. These materials are primarily designed for school-aged children but can be modified for adult learners and some special requests on an individual basis. I would advise registering for a course at least one month in advance (phone: 928-638-7663).[6]

For visitors who want to explore the park individually from their cell phone or tablet, Grand Canyon NP has an official Grand Canyon app for Apple and Android devices. The app is largely accessible for **visitors with access needs** and can be used with speech-to-text, large-text, and reversible-color functions. For **visitors with sight loss**, there is also an online video called *Growing Up at Grand Canyon*, which has audio description and a downloadable transcript (https://www.nps.gov/media/video/view.htm%3Fid%3D1A8EBA6C-1DD8-B71B-0BC16166877E3C10).

Specialized Access

Grand Canyon NP has an accessibility guide with a number of the services that it has available for **visitors with access needs**. You can get a paper copy of this guide from rangers and the information desks at the Desert View Visitor Center, the Grand Canyon Visitor Center, Kolb Studio, the North Rim Visitor Center, Tusayan

Museum, the Verkamp's Visitor Center, and the Yavapai Museum of Geology. Alternatively, you can download a PDF of the guide before you visit the park, although it should be noted that it is not always accessible to screen readers (https://www.nps.gov/grca/planyourvisit/upload/GRCA-Accessibility-Guide-2018.pdf).

OLYMPIC, WASHINGTON

Address: 600 E. Park Avenue, Port Angeles, WA 98362

Phone: 360-565-3130

Website: https://www.nps.gov/olym/index.htm

Accessibility website: https://www.nps.gov/olym/planyour visit/accessibility.htm

Washington

Verbal Image

Washington is known as the Evergreen State for good reason. What I remember most about my first visit to this beautiful state is mountains, a glittering ocean, and trees—trees in the mountains, trees on the lowlands surrounding pastures, and forests running into the sea from craggy rocks and beachheads.[1]

Physically, Washington can be said to be a medium-sized state. At its tallest point, it is around 240 miles (around 400 kilometers) from north to south; at its widest, it is around 360 miles (or around 580 kilometers) east to west; and its landmass is over 71,360 square miles (over 185,000 square kilometers).

As Washington is largely forested, rural, and mountainous, its population is mostly gathered in a few urban areas, with the largest of these areas being on or not far from its western coastline. Overall, the population of Washington was a little under 7,615,000 at the time of writing, with its largest city, Seattle, having a population of over 724,300. By population size, Seattle is followed by Spokane, Tacoma, Vancouver (far south of its Canadian namesake), and Bellevue, in order of descending population. Its capital is the much-smaller city of Olympia, which lies at the southern tip of the peninsula of Olympic National Park.

Geographically, Washington lies at the extreme northwest of the United States, with an average elevation of just over 1,700 feet (around 520 meters) above sea level. The shape of its borders on a map is largely that of a long, tall rectangle, with right angles on its northeastern and southeastern borders. To emphasize this geometric design, Washington's northern and its southeastern boundaries are perfectly flat, as is its eastern border.

The Cascade Range that runs north-south bisects the state into a wet western region that borders the Pacific Ocean and a dry eastern region. As the state border approaches the ocean on its western coastal border, however, the boundary line becomes ragged, and on the coast its boundaries are sprinkled with small and large islands and peninsulas. Washington is also home to dormant volcanoes, such as Mount Baker, and lies on the same series of offshore fault lines that run from Central America through California to Alaska in the US. Given these fault lines, it should be borne in mind that Washington is also a part of a major earthquake zone.

Washington is among the most northerly states in the US, with only Alaska being higher. Alongside Montana, North Dakota, and Minnesota, it is also the most northerly state in the US's greater landmass. This northerly status is reflected in its borders: to its north, it connects with the Canadian province of British Columbia; to its south, it borders Oregon; and to its east, it faces Idaho along the whole of its boundary line. To its western border is the Pacific Ocean.

Climate and Wildlife

Despite its fault lines and dormant volcanoes, Washington is climatically easier to visit than most other states in this book, as it is temperate and largely regulated by its Pacific coastline. Consequently, it tends neither to get too hot nor too cold in the western regions of the state. However, as I wrote above, the Cascades tend to change its eastern temperature, and this range and the plateau to its east are certainly the coldest areas in the state.[2]

Importantly, Washington averages more than seventy clear days of sunshine per year, with an average temperature of a little over 48 F (more than 9 C), an average summer temperature of around 64 F (just under 18 C), and an average winter temperature of around 33 F (a little under 1 C). However, like everywhere else in this book and because of its radically different high spaces, it is prone to very different temperatures in different parts of the state.

In particular, Washington's record high was around 118 F (that is, just under 48 C) in Wahluke in July 1928, and again around Ash in August 1961. By contrast, its record low temperature was around –48 F (around –44 C) in December 1968 in Mazama and Winthrop, at a height of around 1,765 feet above sea level.

A similar picture is painted by the rain and snowfall in Washington, with an average annual snowfall of only three days, with the average snow depth only 5 inches (just under 13 centimeters), whereas the state's average annual rainfall is very high at over 38 inches (which is almost 1 meter).

This rain is, of course, more powerful the closer you get to the coast, with the rain shadow region of the Cascade Mountains getting only an average annual rainfall of around 6 inches (more than 150 millimeters). By contrast, the very aptly named rain forests on the western side of the Olympic Peninsula, which form part of the national park, have an almost unbelievable annual average of 160 inches of rain (which is over 4 meters).

Washington's wildlife is no less spectacular than its rugged green environment. The state's wildlife includes black bears, cougars, deer and elk, hardy mountain goats, Olympic marmots, both bald and golden eagles in its mountain areas, Canada geese and cormorants, the beautiful great blue heron, pileated woodpeckers, the elegant Rufous hummingbirds, and spotted and snowy owls. Its waterways are also well stocked with grayling, sturgeon, trout, and Pacific salmon, and farther out from shore you can find its iconic killer and humpback whales. As I wrote above, Washington's forests are a large part of its landmass and are as diverse as the rest of its geography, and these forests are particularly known for Douglas fir, Sitka spruce, numerous species of pine, and red cedar.

Olympic National Park

Verbal Image
This is a quiet, shy national park that is not as famous as most but is vast at over 922,650 acres of mountains, lakes, rain forests and regular woodland, rapid rivers and streams, and wilderness. It also has a dramatic coastline. In this respect, Olympic National Park[3] (Olympic NP) on Olympic Peninsula is unique, with Puget Sound to the east and the Pacific Ocean to the west, although only a small stretch of the park lies on this coastline.

Despite its vast wilderness areas both immediately outside and within its vast boundaries, it is not too far from many of the West Coast cities. It is just over 110 miles and a little over two hours' drive from Seattle to the east and a little under 170 miles and almost three hours' drive from Portland, Oregon, to the south. Given its temperate climate, the park itself is open permanently all year-round, and at the time of writing averaged around 3,400,000 annual visitors.

Port Angeles is the largest city on the Olympic Peninsula and serves as the northern gateway to Olympic National Park and the

Olympic Mountain Range. Outside the park, Port Angeles can be a good staging point for visiting the park if you are looking for something safer, and it has accommodations, eating and drinking places, and road access to different areas of Olympic NP.

Despite its different wildlife and its Pacific ranges being taller than their East Coast cousins, Olympic NP is at least in part comparable to Acadia on the East Coast, as it is composed of forests and mountains and a stunning, rugged coastline. However, residents of both may disagree, and this is where the comparison ends, as the park is part of the Pacific Coast mountain ranges. This range is, as I wrote above, formed by major offshore fault lines with high-lying fossils, basalt, sandstone, shale, and almost 245 mountains in this Olympic Mountain range, although not all these are in the national park.

Olympic NP's highest mountain—in fact, the highest mountain in Washington State and the provider of the park's name—is Mount Olympus, which stands around 7,980 feet above sea level and around 35 miles from the nearest coastline. Mounts Anderson, Constance, and Deception are among Olympic NP's other tall mountains that stand over 7,000 feet above sea level, with other mountains in this range including Mounts Cameron, Duckabush, Queets, and Christie, as well as McCartney Peak.

Olympic NP also has the third-largest glacial system on the mainland in the United States, with around sixty glaciers, including the wonderfully named Blue, Hoh, Hubert, and Jeffers Glaciers, to name only a few. Farther west on its coastline, the park has an over-70-mile-long gray pebble and coarse sand coastline facing straight onto the Pacific Ocean and lined with loose timber washed up on shore. Out to sea, you'll also see small islands lined with trees, raging waves, and, behind the beaches, cliffs that lead into cool rain forests.

Getting Around Olympic

For almost all visitors to Olympic NP, getting to and around the park must involve an automobile, although the park itself has very little roadway inside its boundaries. The major road that runs all the way around the park is Highway 101, although this only dips into the north of the park as it leaves Port Angeles and enters the Elwha entrance of the park. On the coastal section of Olympic NP, only Highway 110 and the smaller Hoko Ozette Road take you to these sections, with both terminating by the coastline.

In the park, US Highway 101 follows the route of an earlier road around Lake Crescent, which itself was built in the early 1920s. At the time of writing, this section of road was being updated and mended considerably and is still causing long-term disruption. Unfortunately, it is still unknown how long this disruption will last. Furthermore, it should be borne in mind that weather is very unpredictable in this section of the park, meaning that the road is not always travelable. Subsequently, before you travel Highway 101 or any other roads in the area, it is best to check the Washington Department of Transportation Traffic Alert website: https://www .wsdot.wa.gov/traffic/trafficalerts/. Alternatively, I would advise contacting Olympic National Park Visitor Center for information about the park's road conditions prior to setting off (phone: 360-565-3130 or 360-565-3131).

For walkers, being mountainous, partly coastal, rain-forested, and wilderness, Olympic NP's trails can be variable, with many being rough, slippery, and rocky. Walkers should also be aware that some trails can start easily and get rapidly difficult, so you should be cautious when walking no matter what your skill or fitness level. Furthermore, when walking on the park's beaches, visitors are advised to be aware of tide times and heights when trudging the shoreline, and should check the tidal charts at ranger stations and visitor centers in the main part of the park.

Given its position and level of challenge to many visitors, walkers in Olympic NP must also be aware of changing weather even on short hikes. In addition, apart from service animals, you should also be mindful that pets are not allowed on almost all trails in the park, and on the few they are allowed on, they should be leashed at all times, as apart from other dangers, they can be scared by the extreme weather.

Examples of some of the more accessible trails in Olympic NP are the **Cape Alava Trail** and **Sand Point Trail**, which are partly boardwalk from near the ranger station to the coast. On **Hurricane Hill**, which starts as the Hurricane Ridge Road peters out, the trail is largely accessible to **visitors with mobility access needs** on its opening stretch. However, you also need to be aware that after this first section, the trail is largely rough and steep. **Madison Falls Trail** has a short largely accessible section of trail that begins close to the Elwha Entrance Station. This trail also has a parking lot and largely accessible bathroom. The **Spruce Railroad Trail** has a long section of paved trail, too, which is largely accessible to **visitors with mobility access needs**.

Visitors planning to travel around by boat should be aware of strong currents, high waves, rapidly changing weather and temperature, and water temperatures that are often below 50 F, making the risk of hypothermia frequent. If you plan to use a boat in any season, at the very least be sure that the pilot has attended the mandatory Washington State Boating Education Course and obtained a boating education card. In addition, you need to wear a life vest and have the proper safety equipment that is required by law.

Kayakers and canoers planning on traveling in the wilderness sections of the park also need a park permit, and you should be aware that only nonmotorized boats are allowed in the park's wilderness areas at any time. Canoes and boats must be carried on trails by foot, and the park advises looking on the USGS website for specific river conditions at different times if you are planning to paddle through the river system. For those who take this route, you should always stop by a ranger station to inquire about any closures.

In the few places you can use regular motorboats, you should remember that other types of motor craft, such as powered skis, are banned in Olympic NP by Washington State boating regulations. Furthermore, all kinds of motorboat journeys are only allowed in certain restricted areas of the park and are not allowed to land in the park from the north bank of the Hoh River to Makah Indian Reservation.

Visitors planning to water ski can only use parts of Lake Crescent and Lake Ozette. Furthermore, freshwater boat fishing is only allowed on the Ozette River and parts of Queets, Quillayute, Dickey, Quinault, and Hoh Rivers or Lake Crescent and Lake Ozette. Similarly, seawater boat fishing is only allowed on the coastal area of Hoh River. All forms of boat fishing are only allowed in-season, and I would strongly advise contacting the park on their main number for dates and conditions of fishing (phone: 360-565-3130).

Olympic's Facilities

As Olympic NP has few sections of road and is difficult to travel through, it has sparser facilities than most parks. Among its most popular centers are **Olympic National Park Visitor Center** (3002 Mount Angeles Road, Port Angeles, WA 98362, phone: 360-565-3130). This center has educational programs and information with a concession store and is open most days of the year.

For **visitors with sight loss**, exhibits on the park's natural and cultural history include a number of touchable displays, some with Braille and sound effects. For **visitors with hearing loss**, the park orientation video, which is a little under half an hour long, has closed captioning available, which you can ask about at the information desk of the visitor center. In addition, assisted-listening devices are available at the information desk for use in the educational exhibitions. For **visitors with mobility access needs**, a wheelchair is available for checking out at the visitor center, although numbers are limited, and the chairs cannot be booked, so their availability isn't guaranteed. In addition, Olympic NP also offers largely accessible parking and accessible restrooms.

The **Wilderness Information Center** (which is also the Backcountry Permit Office), in the Olympic National Park Visitor Center (3002 Mount Angeles Road, Port Angeles, WA 98362, phone: 360-565-3100), has information and trip-planning advice for wilderness visitors, including trail reports and safety, weather, and Leave No Trace tips. The center also issues wilderness camping permits, which visitors collect from Port Angeles or South Shore Lake Quinault Wilderness Information Center.

The **Hoh Rain Forest Visitor Center** (18113 Upper Hoh Rd., Forks, WA 98331, phone: 360-374-6925) has visitor information, educational exhibits and programs, and concession stores for park goods and books. Outside the center, there are also two self-guided nature trails, and the Hoh River Trail starts nearby. In the summer, rangers also offer guided walks and talks around the local area. Visitors can ask about these when they visit the center and see the talks timetable online on the park's website.

For **visitors with mobility access needs**, the center has largely accessible restrooms, as well as general information, a bookstore, and exhibits on the temperate rain forest. There is a borrowable wheelchair, although this is limited, and availability cannot be guaranteed. Outside the visitor center, the Hoh Picnic Area also has largely accessible bathrooms and one accessible picnic site with table extensions. For **visitors with sight loss**, the center has a number of touchable exhibits and features.

Kalaloch Ranger Station (156954 US Highway 101, Forks, WA 98331, phone: 360-962-2283) is small in comparison to the main visitor center, but it has visitor information about the coast, the settlement of Forks itself, and other areas on the west side of the Olympic Peninsula. It also has a concession bookstore. The station is also a staging point for guided walks and talks about the area around the station. Visitors should be aware that these walks and talks are seasonal.

If you need medical assistance in the park or you need permanent medical support, below are medical centers or places that can be reached or that can provide remote treatment. It should be borne in mind that as the closest medical centers are in towns and villages around the park, and much of the park is wilderness, mountainous, or rain forest, getting to these centers can be problematic.

The centers include:

- **Olympic Medical Center** at 939 Caroline Street, Port Angeles, WA 98362. Phone: 360-417-7000. Website: www.olympicmedical.org.

- **Forks Community Hospital** at 530 Bogachiel Way, Forks, WA 98331. Phone: 360-374-6271.

- **Peninsula Children's Clinic, Children's Hospital** in Port Angeles at 902 Caroline Street, Port Angeles, WA 98362. Phone: 360-457-8578.

- **Bruce Skinner and Associates** at 928 Caroline Street, Port Angeles, WA 98362. Phone: 360-457-1059.

Lodges and Campgrounds

There are lodges, rustic cabins, historic hotels, and motels around the park run by concessioners and often located in Port Angeles, so these won't be discussed here. However, if you want to make a reservation in one of these places, the park advises making reservations in advance as they can fill up quickly. I would personally recommend booking six months or so in advance, if possible.

If you camp in Olympic NP, you must use one of the official campgrounds. There are a number of these campgrounds around the park, although their facilities are often basic, as this park is meant for people who are used to walking trails and being in the wilderness. For instance, there are no showers in the campgrounds and limited cooking water and washing facilities. There is no electricity for those using tents or RVs. The park warns that campgrounds can close quickly when the weather or conditions in the park become unsafe, so even if you've booked, you'll need to check this information before you travel. In addition, campgrounds in the park also have quiet hours between 10:00 p.m. and 6:00 a.m., and during this quiet time, you cannot have night walks. For more information, phone 360-565-3131.

A number of the campgrounds can be reserved before you visit, and at the time of writing these included **Kalaloch, Mora, and Sol Duc** campgrounds (phone: 360-565-3100). You can arrive on the day and try to get into the other campgrounds at Olympic NP, so their spaces, particularly in summer, are not guaranteed. Most of the campgrounds in the park can take RVs, although as the roads are difficult, the height of these RVs in most campgrounds is limited to 21 feet, and some campgrounds only allow lengths up to 35 feet. This being said, vehicle camping is only allowed in authorized campgrounds in the park, with the following being examples of campsites available throughout the park.

Kalaloch Campground (phone: 360-962-2271) is limited with only pit toilets; limited water supplies, particularly in bad weather; little parking access; and no ways of getting to the beach.

Sol Duc Campground has similar facilities to Kaloch, although it has vault toilets and water from the close-by ranger station and only allows organized groups to camp. Reservations for these sites can be made at http://www.recreation.gov or by calling 877-444-6777.

Deer Park Campground is high up in the mountains at 5,400 feet above sea level and is surrounded by steep and snaking rough access roads. This means that visitors can't take RVs to this space. The campground is also only open in the summer, closing in early fall as the weather conditions make visiting difficult at best and often inaccessible. This campground also has pit toilets and no cooking water, but it is said to be accessible to **visitors with mobility access needs**.

Fairholme Campground is on Lake Crescent and as such is often where visitors start boat journeys. Smaller and regular-sized RVs are also allowed onsite, although the campground is only open in high summer and fall and does not take reservations. The site is largely accessible to **visitors with access needs** and has bathrooms and fresh water.

Graves Creek Campground is in the Quinault Rain Forest and open throughout the year, although campsites can't be reserved. The campground is largely accessible to **visitors with access needs**, but because it is in a rain forest with very basic roads, RVs are not allowed, it has no running water, and it only has pit toilets.

The comfortingly named **Heart O' the Hills Campground** is based in the forest and runs summer ranger programs. The campground is open all year round, can take small and regular-sized RVs (although the campground points out there is no dump station), and is largely accessible to **visitors with access needs**. The campground is also prone to snowy conditions and is less accessible when there is snowfall.

Hoh Campground is on the Hoh River and the Hoh Picnic Area. The campground is open throughout the year, and the campground allows small and regular-sized RVs (although no dump stations), has largely accessible bathrooms and running water, and has limited accessible space for **visitors with access needs** for camping and having picnics.

North Fork Campground is small and buried deep inside the Olympic NP rain forest far away from human activity, even in this wilderness area. As such, it has no running water and only pit toilets. However, the campground itself is partly accessible for **visitors with access needs**.

Ozette Campground is on Lake Ozette, and is open throughout the year, although it becomes considerably less accessible in bad weather. The campground allows small and regular-sized RVs and is partly accessible to **visitors with access needs**, although it only has pit toilets and basic water sources.

Queets Campground is just off the Queets River. It is open throughout the year but can only be entered on the Upper Queets River Road at the time of writing. This is a relatively basic campground with only pit toilets and basic water supplies; it is not reservable, and you should not take RVs and trailers.

Staircase Campground is open throughout the year, is just off the Skokomish River, and in the summer has ranger programs. The campground is partly accessible to **visitors with access needs**, but this accessibility varies a lot in the summer and winter, with bathrooms and basic water in the summer but not in the winter. The campground also allows small and regular-sized RVs.

Learning Programs and Tours

As with the other parks in this book, Olympic NP has ranger-led programs throughout the park, and many of these are advertised in *The Bugler*, the park's newspaper, although these programs change radically according to the seasons. The URL for this website changes with every edition of *Bugler*, and so it is best to check the home page of Olympic NP for details and the latest link (https://www.nps.gov/olym/learn/news/index.htm). In addition, *The Bugler* has information on conditions seasonal facilities and accessibility.

Olympic NP also offers the "Outdoor Classroom" for younger visitors to the park (https://www.nps.gov/olym/learn/education/index.htm). This program has different topics aimed at different grade levels and is largely offered online initially in preparation for visiting the park, or they can be used in school rooms without the need to visit the park.

I will write more on this below; however, the materials online include worksheets and videos, a number of which are produced by outside organizations, such as the Science Learning Network; this network designs a number of programs for different areas in the northwestern states, not just Olympia (https://www.nwparkscience.org/). Tours and classes can be used in the park or at a distance.

As one example of the Outdoor Classroom, and like Gettysburg NP in the previous chapter, Olympic NP has a large number of self-directed learning opportunities in the park, which are designed as guided tours. Each of the programs is delivered on the web and via telephone and can be studied in the park at the location the topic is based in, where downloaded materials can be read or watched on a mobile device or printed paper worksheets.

Examples of topics available at the time of writing include "Keepers of the Beat," which includes materials by the Science Learning Network; a briefing PDF; and a guide to the site related to the topic being discussed.[4]

Featured Online Learning

As I wrote above, Olympic NP has a learning site called the "Outdoor Classroom." This material was made distance learning during the COVID-19 pandemic, and although these materials can be downloaded and brought to the park, they are also designed as distance-learning materials for use in classrooms anywhere. Most of the materials produced for this program are either video or PDF worksheet, the latter of which is less accessible to screen readers if you are a visitor with vision loss. However, many of the materials can be adapted by educators in their own classroom (https://www.nps.gov/olym/learn/education/index.htm).

In addition to its more formal education courses, Olympic NP also offers an innovative online audio tour of the park that is available via telephone. This can be listened to in the park if you can get a cell phone signal as you walk around, but it is particularly powerful for visitors with visual impairments dialing in from home and experiencing a virtual tour. To get onto a tour, phone 360-406-5056 and select a venue—although the tour will cost normal cell phone charges, so it may be expensive depending on your location and plan.[5]

Specialized Access

Olympic NP also provides general accessible learning support and can adapt programs for young and old **visitors with access needs**. For general information, see the park website at www.nps.gov/olym, or phone 360-565-3130 or TTY 800-833-6388 or 711. I would advise calling or researching information at least three months before your visit, depending on your access needs, in order to make sure you can arrange the support you need.

ROCKY MOUNTAIN, COLORADO

> **Address:** 1000 US Highway 36, Estes Park, CO 80517
>
> **Phone:** 970-586-1206
>
> **Website:** https://www.nps.gov/romo/index.htm
>
> **Accessibility website:** https://www.nps.gov/romo/planyour
> visit/accessibility.htm

Colorado

Verbal Image

Colorado is also known as the Centennial State and is 380 miles east to west at its widest point, is 280 miles north to south at its tallest point, and has a land mass of more than 103,000 square miles (almost 270,000 square kilometers). As with a number of other states featured in this book, the shape of its borders is geometric, but in Colorado's case, it is almost symmetrical and slightly trapezium shaped, with the flat northern border slightly narrower than its parallel southern border. The name Colorado itself is Spanish for "river that is red," after the Río Colorado, as its water course was colored by the sandstone silt from the Rockies—the Colorado River is the same water course that I featured in the chapter on the Grand Canyon.[1]

Colorado's population is not large for its size at only slightly more than 5,500,000 people, although this number is said to be growing rapidly. This population is largely spread throughout its largest cities, including the largest city in the state, Denver, with a population of more than 705,000 in its city limits, followed by Colorado Springs, the fantastically named Aurora, Fort Collins, and Lakewood.

This lack of population density is not unusual for this part of the US, and the state is also bordered by sparsely populated mountainous and desert-clad neighbors. Clockwise from north, neighboring states include Wyoming to its north, rural Nebraska curling around its northeastern borders, Kansas to the east, the panhandle of Oklahoma on its southeastern pointed border, and New Mexico to its south. Utah lies entirely to the west boundary of Colorado and as such can be said to be physically comparable.

Given its high mountainous plains, Colorado is a major agricultural state and a major producer of alfalfa, cattle, onions and potatoes, sheep, soft fruit such as apples and peaches, and wheat. It is also well known for its modern and growing industries such as private aerospace, creative trades, high-tech companies, and science-technology-engineering-and-mathematics-based (STEM-based) industries. It also has an increasing number of young, mobile, and highly educated people moving to the state.

Being synonymous with the Rocky Mountain range, Colorado is one of the highest, most mountainous states in the US with sweet-tasting air and almost sixty mountains over 14,000 feet above sea level. This makes it popular as an outdoor venue, especially for trekking, white-water rafting, and of course some of the most famous ski resorts in the country.[2] These resorts include Breckenridge, Vail, and the internationally famous Aspen Snowmass.

Climate and Wildlife

Given its height above sea level and its clean, cold air, Colorado averages 136 clear days of sunshine per year, with temperatures averaging over 45 F (over 7 C), although this sways between extremes of weather depending on where you are in the state. In summer, the temperature averages a little more than 65 F (over 18 C), and in winter the state has an average temperature of almost 26 F (over –3 C). These extreme temperatures are even more grueling when you examine its state record temperatures, with the record high being almost 115 F (a little under 46 C) in both Las Animas, July 1933, and again in Sedgwick, July 1954. Conversely, its record low temperature was an eye-watering –60 F (around –52 C) in Maybell, February 1985.[3]

These extreme temperatures are also reflected in its average annual snowfall of almost 20 days per year, giving an average annual snowfall of almost 20 inches (over 48 centimeters). This level of snowfall is comfortably higher than its average annual rainfall of almost 16 inches (over 40 centimeters), reflecting the state's arid mountainous and desert environments.

Colorado's mountainous environment is also reflected in its most common wildlife, such as the state's official animal, the bighorn sheep; black bears; elk; mountain lions; and magnificent birds of prey such as hawks, kites, and eagles. Similarly, its lowlands are in many ways defined by its iconic wild horses, many of which were tamed by American Indians in days gone by; the snakes of its vast plains; and ever-persistent prairie dogs.

Similarly, the state's plant life is equally distinctive with bearberries, stunning Colorado blue columbines, giant goldenrods, serviceberries, mountain snowberries, sweetly perfumed Wood's roses, and tree species such as the fantastically named bristlecone pines and quaking aspens, cottonwood, the Colorado blue and Engelmann spruce firs, Rocky Mountain junipers, and subalpine firs.

Rocky Mountain National Park

Verbal Image

Rocky Mountain National Park[4] (Rocky Mountain NP) is defined by its concentration of spectacular mountain peaks, cut through by enormous valleys, passes, and trails that remain open throughout the year. Arguably, its best peaks are either more than or just under 14,000 feet above sea level and include Longs Peak and Mount Meeker in the southeast of Rocky Mountain NP and Hague's Peak in the center-north of the park.

The shape of Rocky Mountain NP is approximately rectangular with rough, natural borders all round, apart from parts of the eastern and western boundaries that are dead-straight flat lines. On a map, the park is almost reminiscent of a long, thin map of France. The park is also large, at more than 265,830 acres, with most of this area being empty mountain wilderness, and beyond its borders and plainly visible from inside, it is surrounded by Roosevelt National Forest.

In terms of its physical geography, Rocky Mountain NP is to the extreme north-center of Colorado, stopping just shy of Wyoming. The park is therefore not close to many cities and urban areas, which makes it a bit less accessible and a bit more cut off than a number of other national parks in this book. The closest big urban area to Rocky Mountain NP is Denver at a little under sixty-five miles and under an hour and a half by road. The park is also just a little over ninety miles and under two hours' drive from Wyoming's capital, Cheyenne, and under 110 miles and around two and a quarter hours by road from Laramie, Wyoming. Consequently, Rocky Mountain NP can be challenging to get to, in the winter in particular.

Rocky Mountain NP is also surrounded and bisected by large bodies of fresh water, which add considerably to a visit to the park. On its southwestern borders are Shadow Mountain Lake and Lake Granby, and on its northwestern border is Long Draw Reservoir. Within the park, there are a number of smaller bodies of water that trap the melting snow as it flows down from the high peaks, and these include the small but no less remarkable Bear Lake. This water also often defines the shape of the landscape, especially the gorges and valleys in the park, and it provides activities during the warmer months, with many of the rivers being popular for white-water rafting.

The park is also said to have around 300 miles of developed and rougher trails, or, for those who cannot or do not want to walk and climb, many miles of Highway 34 that runs through the north of the park before dropping down over its western side. Highway 34 also runs through the main entrance, the East Entrance, on the northeastern border of the park.

Possibly the most well-known section of Highway 34, with arguably its best views, is the Trail Ridge Road, which is around 12,000 feet above sea level at its highest points. At all points of the park, however, you can see amazing and unique wildlife, plants, and trees, along with peaks and wooded land and very clear nighttime skies with star shows.

Not far outside its eastern borders are Mary's Lake and Lake Estes, and not far off its southwestern border are the splendidly named Windy Gap and Willow Creek reservoirs. Rivers such as the Big Thompson River, North Saint Vrain, and Cache la Poudre flow quickly through the center of the national park. Likewise, although it is not within its boundaries, the Colorado River runs out of Lake Granby and onward to the Grand Canyon to the southeast of the park.

Given its terrain and the extremes of its climate in winter, Rocky Mountain NP's other popular activities include snowshoeing, which you can do with park rangers; cross-country skiing; and sledding. These winter sports are usually staged in the Hidden Valley Ski Area, although it is best to check on weather and environmental conditions before planning or visiting this part of the park in winter as it gets extremely hazardous this time of year. There are also con-cession equipment-rental sites, but, as always, these are beyond the scope of this book.

Getting Around Rocky Mountain

As with many similar parks featured in this book, especially those with vast expanses of wilderness, Rocky Mountain NP has its own free shuttle buses in the summer months, although you should check with the park about the beginning and end of its season. These shuttles are largely accessible to **visitors with mobility access needs,** can accommodate wheelchairs inside, and have lowered floors or lifts to board the buses.

As I have written on other parks' transport systems in this book, you will be strongly encouraged to ride these buses by the National Parks Service. These buses will help preserve the environment, reduce traffic (which is also linked to reason 1), and be more considerate of your fellow travelers.

Around Rocky Mountain NP, there also a number of concessioner-run bus tours, ranging from short tours to all-day tours. However, as these are commercial organizations, I won't be covering these in this book. Whether they are private or run by the national park, these shuttle buses access a number of popular destinations, campgrounds, visitor centers, and loop trails and roads along the Bear Lake Road corridor and beyond.

Before they make it to the park, visitors should note that shuttle bus services only run on the eastern side of the park and not on Trail Ridge Road, which makes accessing these areas more challenging. There are no bike racks on shuttle buses, and pets are not allowed on, as they also won't be allowed in many parts of the park. Only valid service animals such as seeing-eye dogs are permitted—emotional support animals are considered the same as pets in the national park.

The buses generally start from visitor centers and parking lots, making it wiser to park automobiles and then take the shuttle through the park, although I would also advise that you check the park's website for details before your visit. The shuttles leave around thirty minutes apart from early morning until late evening, although it is best to check with the park about availability, as weather may affect the routes, as does seasonal availability.

For more adventurous visitors, Rocky Mountain NP also has a Hiker Shuttle bus that can be ridden from Estes Park Fairgrounds, where you can leave your automobile in their large parking lot. This bus is run by a concessioner, and the services advertise accessible facilities on the bus, but unlike the park's shuttle, you'll need a paid pass to ride it, and its accessibility can't be guaranteed (phone: 970-577-7477).

Manual wheelchairs are allowed throughout the park and on all trails, although I advise not using them or being really careful on many of the trails, which are rough and high. Powered devices for **visitors with mobility access needs**, such as mobility scooters and powered wheelchairs (what the park calls Electric Personal Assistance Mobility Devices or EPAMDs for short), are allowed on all the sidewalks and parking lots in the park. Powered chairs are also allowed on the following trails: Coyote Valley Trail, Holzwarth Historic Site Access Road, Lily Lake Trail, and Sprague Lake Trail.

I'd check with the park before you visit, as these rules may change and weather may mean that they are not allowed at that particular time. It's also important to note that EPAMDs are banned from other trails around Rocky Mountain NP, as they can be dangerous to their users and cause damage to the park's land.

As I wrote above, the park has over 350 miles of trails, some of which are felt to be more or less accessible to **visitors with mobility access needs**, and others which are challenging to even the hardiest walkers with the best balance. All the trails, even those that are largely accessible, can have dangerous and uneven surfaces. Being a mountainous park, most trails also have gradients, and so you should consider this when planning your route around the park.

The following are said to be more accessible trails, although if you are in a wheelchair, the Rocky Mountain NP strongly recommends you use gloves:

- **Hidden Valley** (9,240 feet), which has largely accessible parking and restrooms, picnic areas with largely accessible picnic tables, and a partly surfaced trail with an easier slope.

- **Bear Lake** (9,475 feet) has largely accessible parking and restrooms. Its half-mile gravel trail goes around the lake, although this can get steep in places so this should be walked or wheeled by **visitors with mobility access needs**.

- **Coyote Valley Trail** (8,840 feet) has largely accessible parking, bathrooms, and picnic tables. Its one-mile trail has packed gravel and takes visitors across the Colorado River into the Kawuneeche Valley.

- **Lily Lake** (8,880 feet) has largely accessible bathrooms, parking, picnic tables, and an accessible fishing pier jutting into the lake. It is a three-quarter-mile gravel circular trail on Lily Lake, but check with the park because others in the area are said to be not accessible.

- **Sprague Lake** (8,690 feet) has largely accessible parking, benches, restrooms, and picnic tables. This trail is a half-mile, good gravel trail that goes comfortably around Sprague Lake, starting as it does from a largely accessible campsite just off the lake.

Rocky Mountain NP, despite its size, only has a single main highway, Highway 34, within its borders, although there are side and loops roads running off it and going to other points around the park. These smaller roads can be of variable quality especially during or straight after winter, and their girth ranges from full roads with asphalt and chippings to dirt roads.

The speed limit on many roads is 25 to 35 mph, as weather conditions can be hazardous and those driving at speed especially damage the local environment. Visitors can also only view beauty spots and stop at or access trails around the park using the pull-off areas, and it's important that visitors *do not go rogue* around the park, as pulling into other areas can put you and other drivers in danger.

Before setting off for the park by road, visitors should also be aware that automobiles over twenty-five feet, especially RVs and buses, or automobiles pulling trailers are not allowed in the park. Old Fall River Road is also described by the park as a narrow and hazardous dirt road, making it particularly difficult to navigate. In addition, the weather can change considerably as visitors climb or descend through the mountain range, so it is wise to be cautious and plan ahead. For information about the conditions in the park, particularly on the Trail Ridge Road, phone 970-586-1222.

Many cyclists bring their bicycles to Rocky Mountain NP and enjoy the challenge of riding around the park and pedaling its steep roads or mountain biking its trails. If you do, you need to be careful and travel single file while obeying all traffic laws. The park also allows privately owned horses and concessioner-led horseback rides. The Rocky Mountain NP web page for horseback riding provides addition details about this activity (https://www.nps.gov/romo/planyourvisit/horses.htm).

Rocky Mountain's Facilities

Alpine Visitor Center (Trail Ridge Road, Grand Lake, CO 80447) is the highest national park visitor center in the US (11,796 feet). The center runs education programs and information, has a wilderness office and nature store, and has park rangers touring the center and its complex, who make themselves available to answer questions on the park. The center has accessible bathrooms and parking spaces and a wheelchair-height visitor information desk that is largely accessible to **visitors with mobility access needs**.

Outside and around the center, there are largely accessible parking spaces in the main lot and largely accessible bathrooms throughout the year when the center can be reached. The visitor center opens throughout the summer, from the beginning of June until early October, although it occasionally has to alter its hours for storms or extreme snow or temperatures.

Fall River Visitor Center (8,250 feet; 3450 Fall River Road, Estes Park, CO 80517) has an accessible information desk at wheelchair height, general information, educational exhibits and programs, and a nature store. The center also has largely accessible bathrooms, spaces in its parking lot with low curbs, and an elevator for **visitors with mobility access needs**. The visitor center is also close to a concessioner restaurant.

Holzwarth Historic Site (Grand Lake, CO 80447) is an early original 1920s ranch. For **visitors with a mobility access need**, the center has largely accessible bathrooms and parking spaces, but the parking lot itself has a rough surface when stepping down from the automobile. The site, especially the interior sections, is also difficult to get to over dirt and looser gravel, especially if visitors are using a wheelchair. In some parts of the ranch, there is a partly accessible half-mile, more-compacted-gravel path that runs to the historic site, but even this is steep in places. In summer, visitors can ride in a golf cart there if they have access needs.

Beaver Meadows Visitor Center (1000 US Highway 36, Estes Park, CO 80517) is in the same complex as the park's headquarters building and at the time of writing is in a temporary trailer out in front of the regular visitor center. Hopefully, it will be more available and accessible when this book is published, although the current pandemic is delaying parts of the restoration of the center.

The center provides information and educational exhibits and programs; it has a lecture and presentation auditorium, park rangers based in the building to provide support and spoken information for visitors, and a nature store. For **visitors with mobility access needs**, there are also largely accessible bathrooms, parking spaces, and a low curb, as well as a wheelchair lift. For **visitors with hearing loss** and **visitors with sight loss**, the park's orientation film is closed captioned and audio described. The original building's auditorium also has an induction loop receiver that is accessible to visitors with hearing aids that have a T-switch.

Kawuneeche Visitor Center (16018 US Highway 34, Grand Lake, CO 80447) has information, education exhibits and programs, a lecture auditorium, and in normal times a nature store—although this is closed at the moment. For **visitors with mobility access needs**, the center also has largely accessible bathrooms, parking spaces, and low curbs. As with the previous center, for **visitors with hearing loss**, the orientation film is closed captioned.

As I wrote above, Rocky Mountain NP is far from many nearby urban areas, meaning that it can be difficult to get support if you have medical needs. Depending on where you are in the park, you should also be aware of the hospital locations if needed, with all but one of the medical centers being in Estes:

- **Estes Park Health** at 555 Prospect Avenue, Estes Park, CO 80517. Phone: 970-586-2317 or 970-586-5894.

- **Timberline Medical Center** at 131 Stanley Avenue, Suite 202, Estes Park, CO 80517. Phone: 970-586-2343.

- **Estes Park Health Urgent Care Center** at 420 Steamer Drive, Suite 101, Estes Park, CO 80517. Phone: 970-577-4500.

- **Salud Family Health Centers**, 1950 Redtail Hawk Drive, Estes Park, CO 80517. Phone: 970-484-0999.

- **Physical Therapy Clinic in Estes Park** at 1191 Woodstock Drive, Suite 2, Estes Park, CO 80517. Phone: 970-236-2535.

- **Middle Park Health—Grand Lake Campus** at 301 Marina Drive, Grand Lake, CO 80447. Phone: 970-557-6044.

Lodges and Campgrounds

Given its position and terrain, Rocky Mountain NP can be a challenging environment to visit, especially for **visitors with access needs,** and as such it is sometimes best to look out for more comfortable as well as less rustic facilities. For visitors who want more comfort, outside Rocky Mountain NP, there are a number of resort sites with facilities.

Resorts include Estes Park at the eastern entrance to the park, where there are the greatest number of medical facilities, and northeast Glen Haven and Drake. To the southeast of Rocky Mountain NP is Meeker Park, Allenspark, and Raymond, and to the southwest near the park's western entrance zone is Grand Lake. Many of these municipalities have hotels, motels, lodges, campgrounds, and other facilities. As before, as these are private concessions and regular companies, I don't discuss these options in this book.

Visitors who want to camp inside the grounds have a number of choices; however, as with the other parks in this book, visitors need to be aware of the rules of camping. For instance, Rocky Mountain NP has quiet hours from 10 p.m. until 6 a.m. Campsites also usually have a maximum stay of seven nights in the summer and fourteen nights from early winter and until spring. In the wilderness campgrounds, visitors need permits for differing numbers of nights depending on the season, with an annual maximum camping time of twenty-one nights.

Visitors to Rocky Mountain NP should also note that in a number of regular campgrounds, visitors with America the Beautiful Access Passes and Golden Age Passes can get half off when camping. Reservations and facilities are also variable, depending on seasons, weather, and environmental conditions, so I strongly advise contacting the park before you visit to get costs and opening times. Contact the Wilderness Office (phone: 970-586-1242, TTY: 970-586-1319).

The following two regular campgrounds in the park have accessible pitches for **visitors with mobility access needs**:

- **Moraine Park Campground** near the Beaver Meadows Entrance on Highway 36 has bathrooms, an onsite host, water, and an amphitheater for ranger talks and presentations. Visitors can make reservations at the campground six months in advance on www.reserveamerica .com or www.recreation.gov/ or by calling 877-444-6777. I would advise contacting the campground when you make your booking to discuss support.

- **Timber Creek Campground** is the only campground in the western region of Rocky Mountain NP and is based by the Colorado River. The campground has a dump station and an onsite host, water, trash collecting, and bathrooms. It also has an amphitheater for ranger talks and programs.

There are other campgrounds in Rocky Mountain NP that are generally less accessible to **visitors with mobility access needs** but have trash collection, an onsite host, water, bathrooms, food storage, and lockers. These campgrounds include:

- **Aspenglen Campground** has ranger presentations and talks at its amphitheater and has parking by tents and family sites and spaces for RVs. The campground is reservable in summer up to six months in advance. Website: www.reserveamerica.com or www.recreation.gov/. Phone: 877-444-6777.

- **Glacier Basin Campground** has an amphitheater for ranger presentations and talks. The campground is reservable in summer up to six months in advance. Website: www.reserveamerica.com or www.recreation.gov/. Phone: 877-444-6777.

- **Longs Peak Campground** is twenty minutes south of Estes Park and is forested but only allows tents. It is also high in the Rockies, so weather can be variable and turn quickly.

In some parts of Rocky Mountain NP, visitors are allowed to camp in the wilderness if they have a wilderness permit. At Sprague Lake Camp, there is a largely accessible wilderness campsite for visitors with mobility access needs. This campground also supports wheelchair users, and even though it is a half mile from parking, it has a largely accessible gravel trail. For reservations on this campground, phone 970-586-1242. Wilderness permits can be applied for from the park headquarters' wilderness office or from the desk at Kawuneeche Visitor Center.

Learning Programs and Tours

As with other parks, Rocky Mountain NP has ranger programs, with its evening programs being particularly popular as they often concentrate on star-watching in the clean, clear air in the Rockies. For **visitors with mobility access issues**, these programs may involve partly accessible trails. Where access isn't possible because of inappropriate trails, Rocky Mountain NP advertises the choice of adapting a program, given enough prior notice. For **visitors with hearing loss**, borrowable assisted-listening devices can also be requested for a ranger program, although the park asks for the request to be made three days before attending the program. I would advise you to call a week before your program, as the number of these devices can be limited (phone: 970-586-1206). In addition, ASL interpreters can be arranged on request, although the park asks that you give them at least one month's notice, as the signer has to be contracted especially for the tour they're interpreting. However, I would recommend giving two months' notice before your visit if you can, as these contracts can be difficult to arrange (phone: 970-586-1206).

Rocky Mountain NP can also arrange free field trips and education programs for whole school classes, and these run from late winter to late fall, leaving out only Thanksgiving and the month around Christmas. These trips and programs can be tailored for different curriculum activities for grades K–12. These programs and trips usually include a four-hour visit with at least one teacher or other appropriate adult for every ten class students unless they are young children, in which case the park recommends one adult for four students. There is a required minimum of seven students to run a program and a comfortable maximum of sixty. The park recommends requesting a program three months before you plan to visit, although it may be safer if you ask for a trip or program six months in advance (phone: 970-586-1338).

Featured Online Learning

Rocky Mountain NP also offers free online distance-learning tours of the park through their Rocky Mountain National Park Education and Outreach team. Like the face-to-face programs, these tours are generally aimed at school classes, although they seem to be adaptable to other groups too. The programs online are live and interactive and take place on a suitable app, such as Zoom, Skype, or Google Hangouts. To arrange for one of these programs, you'll also be asked to have a computer or tablet, either of which should have a webcam, high-speed Internet, and a printer. Contact the park's education program manager (phone: 970-586-1338).

Specialized Access

For **visitors with sight loss**, Rocky Mountain NP can provide brochures in Braille and large print at the Beaver Meadows Visitor Center. Brochures are also downloadable in PDF format; however, these do not always work with screen readers, so visitors will need to check they are compatible with their software (https://www.nps.gov/romo/planyourvisit/brochures.htm).

YELLOWSTONE, WYOMING

Address: PO Box 168, Yellowstone National Park, WY 82190-0168

Phone: 307-344-7381

Website: https://www.nps.gov/yell/index.htm

Accessibility website: https://www.nps.gov/yell/planyourvisit/accessibility.htm

Wyoming

Verbal Image

Although Yellowstone is not wholly in Wyoming, over 90 percent of it is. Nicknamed the Equality State or the Cowboy State, Wyoming is perhaps the most archetypal midwestern state in the US. Most of it is on a plateau, with all the land features and climates you can imagine, from its arid red desert to its massive, snow-covered Yellowstone caldera and everything in between. Physically, Wyoming can be said to be a medium-sized state with a total area of more than 97,800 square miles (around 253,325 square kilometers), of which almost 97,000 square miles (over 250,000 square kilometers) is land and around 820 square miles (over 2,100 square kilometers) is water.[1]

In terms of its physical geography, the state is a geometric, almost rectangular shape, corners being just off 90 degrees, and is around 365 miles (almost 590 kilometers) across and around 265 miles (426 kilometers) tall; it is also landlocked. Moving around its borders clockwise, Wyoming neighbors Montana across the whole of its northern boundary, South Dakota and Nebraska to its eastern boundary, Colorado to the south, and Idaho to the west. Utah wraps itself around its southwestern corner.

Wyoming is said to come from the Delaware American Indian words *Maugh-Wau-Wa-Ma*, which translates roughly as "plains that are large." The state also has a population of around 533,000, which means the main regions of its landmass can be described as largely natural wilderness, mountainous, desert, or used for unintensive agricultural. As it is so spread out, beef cattle farming is by far the largest agricultural activity, and the state is an expanse where ranchers and cowboys still flourish; it also has a large American Indian population and large reservations.

As a largely empty state, its cities are relatively small, with its largest city and capital, Cheyenne, having a population of just over 63,600. Its next-largest cities by population are Casper, at over 58,400; Gillette, at almost 32,900; and the almost legendarily named Laramie, at almost 32,400.

Climate and Wildlife

As I wrote above, Wyoming has much of what the US wilderness can offer; however, its climate tends to be colder and more unpredictable than most, largely because it averages over 200 meters above sea level. Consequently, its weather records are often variable according to the height at which their readings were taken. For instance, in Wyoming, July temperatures can average around 75 F (almost 24 C) to around 90 F (a little over 32 C). By contrast, in

January, similar places average around an achingly cold 0 F (more than −17 C) to around 18 F (a little under −8 C).[2]

Beyond its uneven temperatures, Wyoming is mostly arid with only around 10 inches (just under 255 millimeters) of annual rainfall. By contrast, and because of its height above sea level and its expansive mountains, Wyoming has large snowfalls with a jaw-dropping annual average of around 200 inches (or around 5,080 millimeters) in these higher regions.

The extremes of winter and summer are also reflected in the record high and low temperatures in Wyoming. For instance, Basin had the record highest temperature of a scorching 114 F (over 45 C) in July 1900, while Riverside recorded the coldest temperature at an extreme and earth-shattering −66 F (a little less than −55 C) in February 1933.

Most famously, the wildlife reflects its high lands, its extremes of cold and hot, and the vastness of its wilderness. This wilderness includes emblems of Wild West wildlife such as the iconic bison (which is the state symbol), black and grizzly bears, bobcats, deer, elk, moose, mountain lions, pronghorn antelopes, majestic and untamed wild horses, predatory wolves, and the small but gorgeously yellow Western meadowlark. Similarly, its plants include those found often in deserts and highlands, such as sagebrush, many different species of pine, autumn gold ginkgo, plum trees, Bush's lace, cottonwood, Engelmann spruce, chokecherries, lindens, and sweet Goodland apples.

Yellowstone National Park

Verbal Image
As human firsts go, Yellowstone National Park[3] (Yellowstone NP) has the impressive title of becoming the world's first national park in 1872, and as such its wilderness has now been well preserved for almost 150 years at the time of writing. The area of and around Yellowstone was named by American Indian communities local to what

is now Wyoming in the early nineteenth century. These civilizations described the area according to the color of the sandstone rock along the banks of what became the Yellowstone River in eastern Montana, which runs into what is now the national park.

Geographically, Yellowstone's wilderness is reflected in its isolation from large urban areas. For instance, from Wyoming's state capital, Cheyenne, to Yellowstone is a little under 445 miles or around seven hours' driving. Much closer from Yellowstone are Bozeman, Montana, at just under eighty miles or just under an hour and a half drive, and Billings, Montana, at a little over 170 miles away or around two and three-quarters hours' drive. Perhaps the closest large city to Yellowstone is Salt Lake City, Utah, which is just over 320 miles away or around four and three-quarters hours' drive.

Given its isolation, on the map Yellowstone NP itself is super large with a jagged rectangular shape and an irregular eastern side from above. By landmass, Yellowstone can also best be described as being bigger than the states of Rhode Island and Delaware put together. At its tallest, it is a little under sixty-five miles (over 100 kilometers) from north to south; at its widest, it is almost fifty-five miles (almost 90 kilometers) from east to west; and it covers an area of just over 3,470 square miles (just over 8,990 square kilometers). This is an astonishing area of more than 2,200,000 acres of mountains, forests, plains, and water combined, with more than 900 miles (a little under 1,450 kilometers) of trails.

Geologically, Yellowstone NP is formed around an enormous caldera, that is to say, the crater of a volcano, with the volcano underneath the earth's surface being so large that it is described by some as a super-volcano. Yellowstone NP's caldera was formed by a series of huge explosions roughly 2,080,000, 1,300,000, and 631,000 years ago, giving it what is still a highly active field of geysers. These geysers are hot water springs that are warmed by the volcano and shoot up from the earth to relieve their pressure.

The caldera in what is now Yellowstone NP was, of course, first discovered by American Indians. However, the first non–American

Indians to chart and physically map this caldera were the Washburn Expedition, coming from the early US eastern states in 1870, who reported on what is now Yellowstone NP's Upper Geyser Basin.

In all, Yellowstone NP has around ten thousand hot springs and geysers with the largest, most regular, and famous geysers being given fancy names, such as the Grand Prismatic, Morning Glory Pool, and the legendary Old Faithful. A few of these geysers erupt around three hundred times every year, while others erupt only rarely.

Old Faithful itself is in what is now the southwestern part of the park and erupts regularly around twenty times a day, with each eruption coming roughly seventy-five minutes apart and lasting between one and a half to five minutes. With each eruption, Old Faithful can also shoot scalding hot water 100 to 180 feet in the air, with an average height of around 130 to 140 feet. You don't have to visit the park to see the geyser, however, as its activity is now relayed via webcam on the park's web page (www.nps.gov/yell/learn/photosmultimedia/webcams.htm).

Getting Around Yellowstone

For visitors planning to walk Yellowstone NP, there are many choices of trail from the almost nine hundred miles that are available. However, visitors need to be cautious, as the heights, slopes, and weather conditions, can make walking dangerous if care is not taken, with many of the trails in the park being more than seven thousand feet above sea level.

In addition, given its height, many of the advertised trails can also have ice and snow until early summer, or in more extreme settings in the height of summer. These trails can also cross fast-flowing rivers with freezing temperatures, some of which can be around twenty-five feet wide and between three and six feet deep in places. For this reason, it is important to check with the visitor centers before you start walking, for a backcountry situation report.

Many trails in Yellowstone NP begin in the canyon and are interpretive rangers' hikes, although many of the walks are hard and have variable accessibility for people with mobility access needs. Consequently, the park recommends that whenever visitors walk, they also need to exercise extreme caution and carry rain clothes, safety equipment, and a good supply of food and water in case they get trapped or isolated. Walkers also need to be aware that many of the trails are in the wilder sections of the park with few hard surfaces, and there are a great many bears even near the Canyon Visitor Education Center.

Given its size and isolation, the main way of getting around Yellowstone NP is via automobile. There are some concessioner-run shuttle buses, and these include rides such as the Indian Creek Shuttle and the Snowcoach, the latter of which travels from a local, privately run hotel three times a day when the park is open and commutable. There are also a large number of private licensed tours that travel through the park; however, as these are private, I am not going to write about them in this book.

As you might expect for a park as popular and well-known as Yellowstone NP, most roads are almost always crowded, and the distance between the various well-known sites is often arduous. For instance, it is around fifty miles (around eighty kilometers) by road from Old Faithful to Yellowstone NP's impressive Grand Canyon. What is more, after driving these long distances, you'll most often find crowded parking, so it is good to plan ahead to find times that are less popular to visit the park.[4]

Yellowstone NP also has strict road laws, and given its extreme temperature changes and other climatic disruptions such as ice and snow, it also has an almost constant annual road reconstruction program. In the park, visitors must stick to speed limits that are mostly 45 mph, as automobiles often face snaking roads in high areas, changing weather, and extreme inclines. Visitors should also be aware that the maximum length for automobiles (including trailers) is seventy-five feet long.

Yellowstone NP has five road entrances, which are far apart from one another, and your choice of entrance usually points you to what you want to see when you visit. Most of the park's internal road system, however, is closed to regular vehicles from early November to mid-April because the dangerous weather in this area makes running a regular automobile, even with tire chains, almost impossible. After these roads close, only snowmobiles and the appealingly named snow-coaches can make their way around the park on a regular basis.

Given its size, Yellowstone NP has a number of choices of direction visitors can travel via automobile and a number of main highways in, out of, and through the park. The main road systems are highways 14, 191, 89, and 296. When in the park, the main way of getting to the most famous sites is the Grand Loop Road, which connects with highways 20, 14, 212, and 89. The slightly more isolated Norris Canyon Road in the park connects with highway 89 but is closed in winter.

One highway that is open throughout the year, however, is the road from the North Entrance at Gardiner, Montana, which ends at Cooke City, Montana. To check for road conditions, the following websites are said to provide reliable and up-to-date information within their state boundaries: in Idaho (https://hb.511.idaho.gov/), in Montana (http://www.mdt.mt.gov/travinfo/), and in Wyoming (http://www.wyoroad.info/).

Yellowstone's Facilities

Yellowstone NP's visitor centers are long established and have generally good access. As the park is so large and the nature of the park attracts visitors for specific activities—for instance, some people come for the geysers alone, others come to walk the trails, while some come for the wildlife—the experience at each visitor center is distinct. Unlike many other parks in the system, there is no single, overall visitor center for Yellowstone, as its experiences are so wide and diverse. The following is a range of visitor centers that offer particular types of accessibility for **visitors with access needs** and offer specific information about the park, although Yellowstone also has many other good centers and museums, so this is not an exhaustive list.

Yellowstone does not have a central area or a central visitor center, but because of its popularity, the area near Old Faithful is perhaps the most developed area of the park with the fullest range of facilities. Apart from the Old Faithful geyser itself, which has access around for people with mobility access needs, the area also has an inn, a lodge, and stores, although these are concessioner facilities and so won't be covered in this book. However, because this area is much busier than the rest of the park, it has larger parking lots.

Old Faithful Visitor Education Center has information about the park and educational exhibits about the geology of the geysers and the surrounding area of the park. Its exhibits are generally accessible as they are multisensory; there is a general information desk where you can get information about the park and the local concessions. Importantly, there is also information on the predicted geyser eruptions and the conditions in the local area both on signs and screens. For more information, phone: 307-344-2751, or you can follow the center on Twitter, where geyser and environmental conditions are posted regularly (Twitter: @GeyserNPS). For **visitors with hearing loss**, in common with many of the other centers in Yellowstone NP, the films shown at the center often have open captions and there are borrowable listening devices at the information desk.

Albright Visitor Center is on the Grand Loop Road and was once part of Fort Yellowstone, a military installation from the nineteenth century when the park was new. The center has information and educational exhibitions on wildlife and natural history and a store with park goods. For **visitors with hearing loss**, the center is well set up with a number of videos with open captions and borrowable assisted-listening devices for tours and educational programs, as well as an induction loop, which can be arranged at the information desk. For **visitors with sight loss**, the center has a number of touchable exhibits.

West Yellowstone Visitor Information Center is based in the park's local chamber of commerce and is important because it issues a number of permits and passes for the park. It is also close to other local facilities, has a National Parks Service desk, and has information not just about the park but also the local area and concession facilities.

As I wrote above, the canyon area of the park is distant from the geyser area and is a long ride or drive to get to, so for this reason many visitors do not tour the same facilities in a single day. However, although not as well-known as the area around Old Faithful, the Grand Canyon of the Yellowstone River is no less spectacular and has a number of accessible facilities.

The **Canyon Visitor Education Center** is based in Yellowstone NP's own Grand Canyon and has information on the local area and educational talks and exhibits on the geology of the area, particularly Yellowstone's caldera and super volcano. The center also has a theater, bathrooms that can be used anytime of the day, and a bookstore. For **visitors with hearing loss**, the center has a loop system, a number of the films shown in the center have open captioning, and the information desk has borrowable assisted-listening devices for talks within the center. For **visitors with mobility access needs**, the center is largely accessible and has borrowable wheelchairs. For **visitors with sight loss**, a number of the educational exhibits are touchable and multimedia, and there is audio description for films in the theater that can be arranged at the information desk.

Examples of features in the canyon area include the Upper and Lower Falls of the Yellowstone River, Uncle Tom's Trail, and in the canyon itself, the Canyon Village. For **visitors with mobility access needs**, there are largely accessible bathrooms in the parking lot of Brink of Lower Falls and Artist Point. In addition, there is accessible parking on the north and south rims, the designated viewing areas around the canyon, and at the Brink of Upper Falls.

For walkers, parts of the North Rim Trail are generally accessible for **visitors with mobility access needs** and have viewpoints nearby. For instance, one of the viewing areas at Artist Point is generally accessible. At the time of researching this book, several other facilities had just had or were having access facilities installed, as they were in a cycle of general upgrade; however, at the time of writing, I have no more information on these upgrades. Examples of sites being upgraded include Inspiration Point, Brink of Upper Falls, and the South Rim. For more information, phone 307-344-7381. Yellowstone NP has a trail guide of this area that includes information on accessibility.

Perhaps because of its size and its distance from large urban areas, Yellowstone is much like Denali (see chapter 4), for visitors who need to be particularly aware of medical facilities. If you need medical assistance in the park or you need permanent medical support, the following are medical centers or places that can be reached in certain parts of the park:

- **Old Faithful Medical Clinic** at 495 Old Faithful, Yellowstone National Park, WY 82190. Phone: 307-545-7325.

- **Lake Clinic** at 1 Lake Station, Yellowstone National Park, WY 82190. Phone: 307-242-7241.

- **Mammoth Clinic** at 108 Grand Loop Road, Yellowstone National Park, WY 82190. Phone: 307-344-7965.

However, you need to be aware that, as I wrote above, the distances to these facilities may be great, and getting to medical facilities outside the park will involve a long journey.

Lodges and Campgrounds

Concessioners operate a number of lodges in Yellowstone NP, and these are open from late spring through fall. As these are commercial concessions, I will not be writing more about these lodges in this book, but some advertise rooms and facilities, such as food outlets, that are accessible to people with access needs.

There are also a number of campgrounds around the park, and their facilities are diverse and seem to cater to visitors who want varying experiences in the park, from those who want to view geysers to those who want a full wilderness experience. The following campgrounds have accessible features.

Madison Campground is on the South Entrance Road (e-mail: reserve-ynp@xanterra.com; phone: 307-344-7311 or TDD: 307-344-5395; accessibility website: http://www.nps.gov/yell/planyour visit/madisonaccessibility.htm). This campground is well into the park and is around 6,800 feet (over 2,070 meters) above sea level, a little under fifteen miles from West Yellowstone, and a little over fifteen miles from the Old Faithful area. It is also near the confluence of two rivers and has scenic views. For **visitors with mobility access needs**, the site advertises wheelchair access with largely flat and solid trails and paths and reservable accessible sites that have accessible eating and cooking facilities, although it has no accessible shower facilities. I would strongly recommend booking these facilities at least three months or, if possible, six months in advance, as their number is limited.

Canyon Campground is close to being central to Yosemite and not too far from Lodgepole Forest and Canyon Village (e-mail: reserve-ynp@xanterra.com; phone: 307-344-7311; TDD: 307-344-5395). It is also around 7,900 feet (just under 2,410 meters) above sea level. Accessing the campsite by automobile is quite easy, and the campground itself is just off the Grand Loop Road. The campground has a few accessible sites with accessible eating and cooking areas, with largely accessible bathrooms just off the campground. The campground also has access for **wheelchair users and other visitors with mobility access needs**, with largely compacted pathways and trails on flatish ground.

Bridge Bay Campground is also just off the Grand Loop Road and next to Bay Marina off Yellowstone Lake (e-mail: reserve-ynp@

xanterra.com; phone: 307-344-7311; TDD: 307-344-5395). The campground is for water enthusiasts and like Canyon Campground is high up, at around 7,800 feet (almost 2,380 meters) above sea level. For **visitors with mobility access needs**, there are a number of accessible sites with eating and cooking spaces. There are also largely accessible bathrooms within the campground and close by picnic area. As with the other featured campgrounds, there is access for **wheelchair users and people with other mobility access needs** around the campground, with compacted natural pathways and trails. In addition, the campground also has spaces for RVs and automobiles with trailer sites. However, the number of all these spaces is limited, so I'd advise contacting the park and making reservations at least three months in advance, if possible.

Learning Programs and Tours

Yellowstone NP has a number of well-resourced and highly developed ranger-led programs, ranging from talks inside visitor centers to outside tours to talks in campgrounds.[5] In common with a number of other parks in the system, it also runs a series of evening ranger programs, which at the time of writing began close to the end of May and finished in early September.

In addition to those ranger-led activities aimed largely at adults, there is also ranger-led education aimed purely at children and young people, called Junior Ranger Activities. At the time of writing, topics for these activities, which were more informal in nature than classroom-based classes, included Wildlife Olympics; Junior Ranger Discovery Program, which can be used to develop early ranger skills; and Arts in the Park, which includes specialist art and photography classes, some of which are with the resident park photographer, Jim Peaco. Venues for these programs change and include exciting spaces such as the Pop-Up Art Studio at Grant Visitor Center or Old Faithful's yurts.

In addition to the park-run programs, there are also a number of concessioner-guided tours that are licensed or authorized by

Yellowstone NP that happen around the park and include specialist activities, from extreme to basic walking tours to photography, painting, and fishing.

Yellowstone NP, through the Yellowstone Forever initiative, also runs a more structured program for younger visitors, which follows a more school-type curriculum and is sponsored by the National Science Foundation. At the time of writing, the park was running self-directed programs, such as Explore as a Young Scientist, that were designed for children five years old and older.

These children's explorer programs are based on a booklet that the park designed and featured mysteries and puzzle-type activities that families followed outdoors and in the visitor centers. Families can get these booklets during their visits from the Canyon Visitor Education Center or Old Faithful Visitor Education Center, and completed booklets can be taken back to these education centers to earn a patch or keychain.

In addition to their family-based activities, Yellowstone NP also runs more formal field institutes and field schools out of the park called Ask a Ranger, which are aimed at classes and groups of children. The institutes and schools are residential programs, although at the time of writing, these had been curtailed because of the COVID-19 pandemic.

Currently, these programs have been developed to engage classes of sixth graders through eighth graders on interactive-map activities and last four to five days, so they represent a substantial visit to the park.

Featured Online Learning

For visitors who cannot get to Yellowstone NP in person, the park runs online programs where children and adults can separately explore different sites and features.

For children, these programs are usually run through school classes, are organized by teachers, and include topics that are on their general curricula, such as cultural history, ecology, and geology.

Each program includes live online discussions and talks by members of park staff, usually rangers, which last between twenty and forty minutes each. In addition to formal curriculum discussions, park rangers can also discuss their careers with classes, which is particularly useful for children thinking of joining the service when they're older.

To book one of these programs, teachers will have to arrange the contents and delivery of each lesson and make a call to the park to help organize their custom program. As this can take a little organization, especially to arrange a ranger to lead the class, I would advise contacting the park to arrange this at least three months in advance.

There are some regulations to these classes and some preparation for teachers. First, classes or groups need to have ten or more children. Second, visitors will have to have their own computers or tablets, either with a separate or built-in webcam; fast and reliable Internet access; and at least one account with FaceTime, Google Hangouts, or Skype. Third, teachers will need specific dates when they want their classes and local times to call. They'll also need to have a general topic they want covered and that can be developed by the Yellowstone NP—a list is given by Yellowstone of topics they normally cover.

For example, some of the themes and topics that previous online tours of the park have covered are animals in Yellowstone NP; the park's geysers, geyser fields, and volcanoes; rocks and other geological features in the park; and the process of preservation in the park, that is to say, how the park preserves wildlife, plants, trees, and its environment. After covering these areas, students in these classes can be presented with a "Virtual Visitor Stamp" by the park in recognition of their work, and this can be printed and added to the park's passport.

Yellowstone NP also has its own app that can be used online and off-line, with much of the educational material found on the park's website. The app not only can be studied at home and has many accessible features for visitors' tablet or cell-phone operating systems, but it also has largely accessible maps and guide publications from Yellowstone. These maps and guides can be brought to the park and used as self-guided tours of the park. The app is available free through Apple's App Store and Google Play.

In addition to its online learning programs and tours, Yellowstone NP also has live-streaming and "static" webcams showing visitors who can't get to the park in person what is happening during all and any times of the day. These webcams are based at the north and west entrances, Mammoth Hot Springs, Mount Washburn, and in the Upper Geyser Basin. The website with the webcams was developed by the Eyes on Yellowstone program, funded by Canon USA, Inc., and also has a map that pinpoints which part of the park the visitor is viewing (https://www.nps.gov/yell/learn/photosmultimedia/webcams .htm). As a part of this program, you can also watch Old Faithful live (www.nps.gov/yell/learn/photosmultimedia/webcams.htm).

Specialized Access

For **visitors with sight loss**, Yellowstone NP can arrange borrowable large-print and Brailled versions of Yellowstone NP's maps and some brochures through its visitor centers. I would strongly advise contacting the park before you visit to ask about these accessible maps and guides, or you can simply download a copy in a Braille Ready Format (.BRF) (https://www.nps.gov/yell/planyourvisit/ accessibility.htm). The park also has a downloadable audio description of its map and guides on its website and through its app. These audio descriptions include sites and spaces such as the Albright Visitor Center at Mammoth Hot Springs and Fort Yellowstone National Historic Landmark District.

Visitors with hearing loss can also arrange ASL and other sign-language interpreters for ranger programs, although the park asks that you contact them at least three weeks before you plan to visit to arrange this. However, their availability is scarce, so I'd call at least a month before you plan to visit (phone: 307-344-2251 or TTY: 307-344-2386).

YOSEMITE, CALIFORNIA

Address: Public Information Office, PO Box 577, Yosemite, CA 95389

Phone: 209-372-0200

Website: https://www.nps.gov/yose/index.htm

Accessibility website: https://www.nps.gov/yose/planyourvisit/ accessibility.htm

Deaf Services website: https://www.nps.gov/yose/planyour visit/deafservices.htm

California

Verbal Image

With the small, exquisite city of Sacramento[1] as its state capital, California is known as the Golden State and is the wealthiest and most populated and popular state in the US to live and work in. It is so wealthy that, at the time of writing, it is estimated that if it were a country, it would be just behind Germany as the fifth-wealthiest country in the world. However, its famous urban areas and its even more famous technology, movie, television, and music businesses distract attention from its copious and magnificent wilderness areas. This wilderness includes pretty much most of what visitors should expect in such a large and diverse area, with mountain ranges, forests of giant trees, deserts, craggy shorelines, a petulant ocean, and backcountry taking up most of its environment.[2]

Physically, the total area of California is more than 158,700 square miles (over 411,000 square kilometers). In this area, land takes up almost 156,300 square miles (over 404,810 square kilometers), and inland reservoirs, lakes, and rivers take up almost 2,410 square miles (just over 6,230 square kilometers). At its widest, California also extends around 350 miles (about 560 kilometers) from east to west, and at its tallest, its maximum height is around 780 miles (1,260 kilometers).

As for its physical shape on a map, California is a tall, thin, angled state, sloping geometrically and with a straight-lined border to the east, looking a little like it's been bent in half, and shaped like a wide arrowhead facing west. The state's southern and northern borders are also perfectly straight and horizontal, whereas its western border is simply its ragged coastline. Working our way clockwise on a map, California is bordered to the north by Oregon; to the east by the mountains and deserts of Nevada; and to its southeastern corner by Arizona, where it is separated by the Colorado River. To the south, California is bordered by Mexico's state of Baja California Norte, which takes its name from the same Spanish source as its northern neighbor, and to the west, California is framed by its Pacific Ocean coastline.

Historically, California's name was given by the Spanish conquistadors and taken from a mythological land of paradise called "Califia." This land first appeared in the sixteenth-century novel by Garcia Ordonez de Montalvo entitled *Las Serges de Esplandian*, which was highly popular in the Spanish empire at the time of its colonization of the western Americas.

Today, California's population is comfortably more than 39,500,000, with its five largest cities being Los Angeles (with a population of almost four million), San Diego, San Jose, San Francisco, and Fresno. However, this does not tell the whole story of these cities, as their metropolitan areas stretch way beyond their city limits, with the county of Los Angeles having a far greater population than the city itself. Similarly, the Bay Area that surrounds San Francisco, which includes the legendary Silicon Valley, is so large as to be the second-largest metropolitan area in California, overtaking those of San Diego and San Jose.

Climate and Wildlife

Of course, the first thing that anyone who has traveled around California knows is that the state has very diverse weather that can be cold and rainy to the north, and tropical inland and to its southern border, particularly where it meets Mexico. Consequently, as a whole, California can be said to be a warm state but is kept relatively temperate and stable by its ocean coastline that cools in the summer and keeps warm in the winter. Consequently, year-on-year the state averages around a comfortable 146 total days of sunshine.[3]

Temperature-wise, California has an average summer temperature between just under 60 F (over 15 C) to around 97 F (just over 36 C), whereas its winters have average temperatures of between 40 F (just under 4.5 C) to around a surprisingly cold 15 F (just under −9.5 C). As with many other western states in this book, the diversity of land and climate is reflected in California's record temperatures, with its highest recorded temperature being just under a roasting 135 F (almost 57 C) in July 1913, whereas its record low temperature was around a bitter −45 F (around −43 C) in January 1937.

Perhaps surprisingly, given its average low temperatures in parts of the state, its average annual snowfall is no days of snowfall and 0 days averaging over 0.1 inches. However, it should be borne in mind that this snowfall is an average of the whole state and not its snowiest areas inland, which of course have high levels of snow. In addition, given its long coastline, there is no hiding the rainfall in these averages, and California's annual average rainfall is over 22 inches (almost 565 millimeters).

In terms of its wildlife, California is perhaps best known for the California grizzly bear on its flag, although this species is now said to be largely or completely extinct according to varying reports. There are, however, slews of black bears in the state, and varying land animals depending on where you are, including coyotes, bighorn sheep, desert tortoises, the wonderfully named kangaroo rats, kit foxes, ground squirrels, deer, marmots, mink, mountain lions, ospreys, porcupines, raccoons, skunks, and weasels. California's air is also filled with large numbers of species of butterflies, ducks, geese, jays, kingfishers, bald eagles, owls, and teal.

Perhaps most famous of all California's natural environments are the giant redwood trees that seem to flourish and have been resilient to extreme weather, forest fires, earthquakes, and the other natural disasters that have befallen the state over the centuries. The redwoods even have their own national park in California, and the stately sequoia trees frame the eastern borders of the state in the Sierra Mountains.

Other species that flourish in California include dogwood, willows, laurel, oak, various pines, and alder, the latter of which acts as home to many of its native species of butterflies, as well as Joshua trees, made famous by the rock band U2. Then there are also more delicate plants such as the gorgeous California poppies, ferns, Shaw's agave, hoary California fuchsia, the sweetly named lemonade berry, cacti, sagebrush, and creosote.

Yosemite National Park

Verbal Image
Part of the High Sierra in the Sierra Nevada mountain range, Yosemite National Park (Yosemite NP),[4] can be said to be a large park at a little under 1,190 square miles (3,028.8 square kilometers) or around 750,000 acres. The shape of the park is like a deflating

round balloon with rough edges defining its borders, and the park is surrounded by the Stanislaus and Sierra national forests. Internally, the park features mountains, cliffs, deep valleys, giant sequoias, meadows, waterfalls as tall as small skyscrapers, and a vast wilderness area. The park is also generally easy to travel to and through, having as it does around 360 miles of hard-paved roads. The park gets an average of four million to five million annual visitors.

There is debate about the origins of the name Yosemite; however, a number of sources say that it means "grizzly bear," which were once numerous in the area, or "killers," a term that itself had a disputed root. The only thing that these sources can agree on, however, is that the word comes from a local tribe of American Indians. Prior to being called Yosemite, the area was less controversially named "Ahwahnee," which was another American Indian word meaning "big mouth."

Although Yosemite is not as cut off from large urban areas as some of the other parks I have written about in this book—and of course California has large cities and is surrounded by states with large cities—it is still backcountry US. The closest city is Fresno, which is sixty miles away or an hour-and-a-quarter drive, whereas Los Angeles is almost 280 miles away or four and three-quarters hours' drive, and San Francisco is a little over 140 miles away or almost two and three-quarters hours' drive.

Established originally as an area that required federal government protection in 1864, Yosemite NP became a fully fledged national park in 1890, being only the third to be given this designation. Even today, it remains a largely untamed area of the state, and around 95 percent of the park is designated as wilderness.

From its earliest days in the nineteenth century, Yosemite became a popular destination for education, for artists wanting to escape the cities, and for the leisure of Californians, and it was later made famous by the black-and-white photography of Ansel Adams. Adams's photographs of giant cliffs and waterfalls are now revered worldwide, and many of his prints are exhibited in the Ansel Adams gallery in Yosemite Village.

Perhaps of all the national parks featured in this book, only one or two can be said to have a highly defined visitor area where most people arrive, often do not leave during their stay in the park, or use as a base for exploring. At around eight miles (almost thirteen kilometers) wide, Yosemite Valley is the central point for visitors to the park and has soaring granite walls that at some points are more than twice the height of the Empire State Building.

Much like the Grand Canyon featured earlier in this book, the main features of Yosemite Valley were made over a period of thirty million years by glaciers pushing their way through the rock, weathering, and erosion. This erosion has left a legacy of spectacular natural features the highlights of which include the Yosemite Falls, which is North America's tallest waterfall with a drop of water of around 2,425 feet; the smaller but no less impressive Bridalveil Falls, which drops around 620 feet; the grandly named Cathedral Beach; El Capitan (El Cap), which at almost 3,600 feet tall is the country's tallest granite monolith; and, further into the park's wilderness area, three groves of giant sequoias that are among the world's tallest trees.

Getting Around Yosemite

Generally speaking, Yosemite NP has good internal public transportation, including the open-air Yosemite Valley Floor trams, and although these only stop in the valley, all routes operate throughout the year. **Visitors with mobility access needs** who plan to ride the trams should contact the park to arrange for special provisions; the park asks that they be contacted forty-eight hours or more in advance, to make sure an accessible tram or bus is available (phone: 209-372-4386).

In common with many of the other parks, there are also a number of regular shuttle buses that function as a part of the Yosemite Valley Shuttle System, although times and access vary at different times of the year and according to differing circumstances. For instance, the buses mostly travel from early morning to evening or late evening; however, at the time of writing, these shuttles had stopped because of the COVID-19 pandemic.

The shuttle buses often go to a number of popular sites in the park, the majority of which are in Yosemite Valley and include the El Capitan Shuttle, the Mariposa Grove Shuttle, shuttles to Badger Pass Ski Area, the Glacier Point Tour, the Tuolumne Meadows Shuttle, the Yosemite Valley to Tuolumne Meadows Hikers' Bus, the YARTS Highway 120 east and north buses (these are separate routes, so check with the driver before boarding), and YARTS Highway 41 Bus. These shuttle buses are generally free, except for the YARTS buses, which charge.

For **visitors with mobility access needs**, the shuttle buses are often largely accessible and have wheelchair lifts and secure spaces for wheelchairs to fit. However, visitors wheeling themselves need to take into account that the maximum size of wheelchair these buses can take is 24 inches by 46 inches. **Visitors with mobility access needs** can also ask for assistance from the bus driver, who have been trained to provide support, and the park again advises visitors to contact them up to forty-eight hours before they visit to make sure that the bus on their route is accessible.

For visitors who ride on mules or horses, Yosemite NP has stables at Yosemite Valley, Tuolumne Meadows, and Wawona, and these stables offer trail rides throughout the summer that can be personalized to visitors' preferences. In the Yosemite Valley and Wawona stables, bathrooms are partly or largely accessible for **visitors with mobility access needs**.

The park asks **visitors with access needs** wanting to ride a trail to contact them at least twenty-four hours before visiting, to plan their ride and to explain their access needs so the correct support can be arranged. As this is a specialist support service, I'd advise contacting the park at least one week in advance, if possible, as some requests can take time to arrange (phone: 209-372-8348 for Valley Stables, 209-372-8427 for Tuolumne Meadows Stables, and 209-375-6502 for Wawona Stables; website: www.yosemitepark.com/mule-horseback-rides.aspx).

For walkers and riders who want to travel independently, Yosemite NP is said to have around 750 miles of trail. However, as with all the other wilderness parks in this book, the accessibility on these trails changes markedly depending on weather or environmental conditions or where you are in the park.

One example of a partly accessible trail is the one going from the shuttle bus stop number 6 to the Lower Fall, which the park describes as a paved loop trail that is partly accessible to wheelchairs and runs for a little over one mile. However, even on this trail, walking and wheeling can be challenging as it has different gradients and slippery bridges, but it also has seating areas along the way.

For **visitors with vision loss**, this trail also has a bronze relief map and touchable granite boulders that are set up as educational exhibits along the way. There are also largely accessible bathrooms near the shuttle bus stop itself. From this bus stop, the half-mile western trail is also said to be accessible but more challenging for **visitors with access needs**.

For visitors with access needs who prefer more challenging trails that can nevertheless be dangerous, there is a partly accessible trail on Wawona and Glacier Point Road at the southern end. However, although stunning in parts, this trail is advertised as being particularly challenging to **visitors with mobility access needs**, especially those visitors in wheelchairs. This is largely because its route takes visitors through forested areas with occasionally uneven trails that lead to waterfalls, lakes, and granite features.

All visitors should also bear in mind that when walking or riding through wilderness areas, you'll generally need a permit. You can get information about these wilderness permits by contacting Yosemite NP's main offices for details (phone: 209-372-0200).

For those traveling by automobile to Yosemite NP, there are three highways that travel to the entrance of the park and continue on inside: Highway 41 meets Yosemite from its southern border; Highway 140 is on the western border of the park; and above Highway 140, Highway 120 meets the borders of both the western and eastern entrances of the park and continues via a single highway through the park. In summer, the park also warns visitors that there are congestion and parking problems, particularly in Yosemite Valley. For more relevant information on traveling and road conditions, phone 209-372-0200 followed by #1 and #1.

It is also important to note that Yosemite NP has strict regulations about vehicle sizes, and these regulations vary in different parts of the park to comply with different California road laws and to make it through tunnels. Consequently, if visitors are traveling into the park via RV or you have an outsized automobile such as a bus or are towing a trailer, I would strongly advise checking with the park before you plan your visit. For instance, nothing larger than twenty-six-seater buses or automobiles over thirty feet long are allowed on Glacier Point Road as it passes through the Badger Pass Ski Area and this area can be particularly environmentally dangerous.

Yosemite's Facilities

As I wrote above, Yosemite NP's facilities are centered around Yosemite Valley, and some places are generally seasonally available while a number of others are open all year round if conditions permit. What follows are a number of visitor centers and facilities that are generally more accessible.

Valley Visitor Center in Yosemite Valley is perhaps the closest place that can be described as Yosemite NP's main visitor center, and it has information, educational exhibits, and the Yosemite Valley Theater. At the time of writing, the theater ran free films about Yosemite NP, which in season were shown on the hour and half hour and include *Spirit of Yosemite*, which is on the park's scenery, its natural and human history, and its cultural heritage; and *Yosemite: A Gathering of Spirit*, which is similar.

Visitors with mobility access needs should be aware that the center's exhibitions are in a museum-type space that is largely accessible and has power-assisted doors at front and rear entrances. The center's rear doors also have a ramp, and there are largely accessible bathrooms, paths leading to the center, and parking spaces outside. The shuttle bus leading to the center is also generally accessible. **Visitors with vision loss** have tactile exhibits, including some of the local historical artifacts, and there is a tactile relief map and audio tour. For **visitors with hearing loss**, both films in the theater are captioned, and there is a borrowable transcription of the movie script of *Spirit of Yosemite* at the information counter.

Yosemite Museum has shuttle bus stops outside and what is described as an intermittent art gallery, meaning that it has art exhibits at different times throughout the year and so is largely seasonal. At the time of writing, the museum had the Indian Cultural Exhibit on the Ahwahneechee nation, who inhabited Yosemite Valley prior to Westernization.

For visitors with vision loss, there is a touchable Miwok and Paiute cedar bark house and a cross-section of a Giant Sequoia tree outside. For **visitors with access needs**, there are also generally accessible interpretive ranger programs in or near the museum, although I would advise asking the park about these before you visit so they can arrange support for your specific needs.

The **Indian Village of Ahwahnee** is an outdoors educational center designed to school visitors about the original Ahwahneechee nation in Yosemite Valley, and it has displays about the culture and lives of these inhabitants. For **visitors with vision loss**, the village has a trail with audio buttons narrating different parts of the village.

The **Valley Wilderness Center** isn't a traditional visitor center but can help visitors with their applications for and issue wilderness permits and has information about walking and camping. The center also has self-guided learning materials on the wilderness in Yosemite NP, walks in the park, and how to make a minimum impact on the natural environment while camping in the park.

The **Happy Isles Art and Nature Center** is on the shuttle bus route, has specialist information, and is a family-oriented education center. Outside, a volunteer also narrates the outdoor exhibits and can provide nonspecialist information for **visitors with sensory and learning access needs**. The educational offering in the center focuses on family experiences and park visits and is largely accessible by default, as it has interactive and multisensory as well as traditional natural history exhibits and art workshops.

Not far from the center's building, visitors can follow short trails through the area's forest, fen, and nearby river and also see the remains of the 1996 rockfall from cliffs at Glacier Point. Visitors should note that this is only open from spring through to the beginning of fall, coinciding with the long summer break.

There are two main centers for arts visitors to Yosemite. The **Yosemite Art Center and Education Center** is run by Yosemite Conservancy, is on the shuttle bus route, and offers art classes, some of which can be developed to be accessible (phone: 209-372-1442 or 209-379-2646). In addition, the Ansel Adams Gallery has rolling exhibits on the work of this famous artist, as well as changing exhibits by and education on other important photographers and artists (phone: 209-372-4413; website: www.anseladams.com). For **visitors with mobility access needs**, there is a ramp out front and to the gallery's upper level via an outside path.

Around the park, there are also largely accessible picnic areas, such as East Yosemite Valley, El Capitan Picnic Area, Lower Yosemite Fall, Yosemite Valley, Wawona, Hetch Hetchy Sentinel Beach, Soldier Flat, Swinging Bridge, and Tioga Road. These areas have largely accessible bathrooms, picnic tables, and grills, but visitors need to beware that some areas don't have parking lots.

If you need medical assistance in the park or you need permanent medical support, the following are medical centers or places that can be reached or that can provide local treatment; although it should be borne in mind that, given the size of Yosemite NP, getting to these centers can be problematic. There is one center in the park, **Yosemite Medical Clinic**, which is based in Yosemite Village (phone: 209-372-4637).

Outside Yosemite, you will find the following centers not too far away:

- **C. Fremont Hospital** at 5189 Hospital Road, Mariposa, CA 95338. Phone: 209-966-3631.

- **Northern Inyo Hospital** at 150 Pioneer Lane, Bishop, CA 93514. Phone 760-873-5811.

- **Tuolumne General Hospital** at 101 Hospital Road, Sonora, CA 95370. Phone: 209-533-7100.

- **Horizons Unlimited Health Care**, **Mariposa Clinic** at 5320 Highway 49 North, Mariposa, CA 95338. Phone: 209-966-2344.

- **Sonora Regional Medical Center** at 1000 Greenley Road, Sonora, CA 95370. Phone: 209-536-5000.

- **Mercy Medical Center** at 333 Mercy Avenue, Merced, CA 95340. Phone: 209-564-5000.

- **Valley Children's Hospital** at 9300 Valley Children's Place, Madera, CA 93638. Phone: 559-353-5150.

- **Mammoth Hospital** at 185 Sierra Park Road, Mammoth Lakes, CA 93546. Phone: 760-934-3311.

- Importantly, there is also urgent care in the **Adventist Community Clinic** at 48677 Victoria Lane, Oakhurst, CA 93644. Phone: 559-683-2711.

Lodges and Campgrounds

As you may expect for a park that has developed over a century, Yosemite has well-developed campgrounds and extensive lodging facilities. However, as the lodges are run by concessioners, I'm not going to cover them in this book. Yosemite NP campgrounds have water, and most have regular restrooms. There are thirteen regular campgrounds, seven of which are reservable, while others are wilderness campgrounds with backcountry camping facilities, which means there are no bathrooms or regular water facilities (website: www .recreation.gov; phone: 877-444-6777 or TDD 877-833-6777).

The campgrounds with accessible spaces and water (although some sites have natural water that needs sterilizing) include Upper Pines (which is open all year), Lower Pines, North Pines, Wawona, Crane Flat, Tamarack Flat, Yosemite Creek, Porcupine Flat, and Tuolumne Meadows. Most of these campgrounds also allow RVs, although you'll have to check with the website before you visit to confirm whether they do. The backcountry campgrounds include Little Yosemite Valley and an area not far from High Sierra camps, although you'll need to have a wilderness permit to stay at either site. Finally, there are also campgrounds with facilities for those with horses at Wawona, Bridalveil Creek, and Tuolumne Meadows, although not all of these have access facilities (phone: 209-375-9535).

Learning Programs and Tours

As Yosemite told me on their learning access facilities, "We do not have publicly advertised classes for people with disabilities, although we will lead walks for groups who have disabled members by request. This has been occurring for at least 20 years. Deaf Services frequently offers specialty talks or walks for large Deaf groups."

As is the case with all other national parks in this book, Yosemite NP has a variety of ranger-led programs, and in addition it also runs Ranger Interpretive Programs. These are outlined in the Yosemite Guide and include a series that ranges from campfire programs to talks, which often take place on its campgrounds or in concessioner lodges. A full list of these programs are described on the park's website (www.nps.gov/yose/planyourvisit/guide.htm).

Yosemite NP also has Parks as Classrooms programs for school classes and other groups of children and young people, such as Scout groups. These programs are bespoke and include activities such as field trips. Example topics given by Yosemite NP include ecology, geology, histories of local American Indian nations and communities of later settlers, or the natural history of the park.

These programs are offered on weekdays only in the regular academic year, and sessions will be between one and two hours long. The park asks teachers to contact them and arrange sessions in person at least three weeks in advance; however, as these are popular and time slots are booked quickly, I'd always advise contacting the education department at least two months in advance, if possible (phone: 209-375-9503). The classes can be for upward of thirty students at a time, and visiting classes also need to have one chaperone for every six students.

Yosemite also runs more independent learning classes outside class time that are aimed at families with children. One example is Youth in Yosemite, which is a publicly available, self-directed learning program for visitors ages four to twenty-five years. To find out more about this and similar programs, contact the Education Branch at the park before you visit (phone: 209-375-9503). "Occasionally the park will hire a seasonal [professional] with special training (for example, working with students on the Autism spectrum) and that will be utilized during their season, but there is no hiring specifically for these skills."

Featured Online Learning

For **visitors with hearing loss** who can't get to Yosemite NP or who want to study material before visiting, the park has a range of short, open-captioned films that are designed as public education resources. For example, it has a series of films called *Alaskan Elders: Timeless Tales from the Trail*, and these videos run from just over two minutes to just under six minutes. For more information about these, contact Accessible Learning Support in the Education Office at 209-375-9503.

In common with the other large parks in this book and in the system, Yosemite NP has an official app that can be used on- and off-line and works with the accessible features on cell phones and tablets. The app is sponsored by Yosemite Conservancy, free to download, and available on the Apple App Store and on Google Play. To use it off-line, go to the "Settings" in the app menu and tap on "Download Offline Content." This app includes tours, itineraries, information on visitor centers and getting around the park, schedules, services, and maps, as well as allowing you to save items, create collages, and change its settings. The app also has many features built in for **visitors with access needs**. For example, for **visitors with vision loss**, some of the sites around the park are audio described, including some outdoor exhibits and tactile relief models, and all the images have alternative text.

Specialized Access

In Yosemite, there has been someone in the role for at least 20 years. At this time, Yosemite [has an officer] serving as Coordinator for physical accessibility. . . . The Deaf Services Coordinator is the de facto Programmatic Accessibility Coordinator at this time. . . . The park [now] provides . . .

- The bronze view shed displays throughout the park, as well as the touch display of Yosemite Valley in the visitor center are particularly popular with visitors who are blind.

- The park's bike rental stands have hand-crank bikes for visitors who do not have use of their legs and tandem bikes for visitors who are blind.

- The visitor center museum displays have a descriptive audio tour.

- Deaf Services includes trip planning by videophone, trip planning in ASL at the Visitor Center and an ASL interpreter for park programs. We provide Assistive Listening Devices for visitors who are hard of hearing. We provide disability/accessibility/Deaf Services training and ASL classes, when available.

- Deaf Services Facebook page.

Yosemite NP has an accessibility guide called simply "Accessibility," which can be downloaded on a PDF from the website (https://www .nps.gov/yose/planyourvisit/upload/access.pdf)—although as a PDF it may not work as well on some screen readers. The park has also produced a visual guide to Yosemite Valley for visitors with aphasia. (https://www.nps.gov/yose/planyourvisit/upload/aphasia-guide .pdf). Both these documents can be downloaded from its accessibility web page: https://www.nps.gov/yose/planyourvisit/accessibility .htm.

As I wrote above, Yosemite has had a highly developed, specialized Deaf Services program since the 1970s. This is an award-winning scheme that has been used as a model by many others in previous years (https://www.nps.gov/yose/planyourvisit/deafservices .htm; video phone/text: 209-379-5250).

[Our] Deaf Services program began with a summer seasonal position in 1979 and that position became permanent and year-round in 2016. Yosemite has the first year-round, permanent Deaf Services Coordinator/ASL interpreter-ranger in the NPS.

The Deaf Services position began with Len McKenzie, the Chief of Interpretation at the time, giving an interpretive program. On the walk, he could see there was a Deaf man in a wheelchair and his companion was interpreting for him. He realized he had no way to accommodate Deaf visitors and asked the interpreter, Maureen Fitzgerald, to join the staff for a summer. Maureen invited a Deaf community member from the Bay Area to advise the park on how to best serve Deaf visitors. This led to the establishment of the earliest Deaf Services program in the park service.

Examples of Deaf Services activities include sign language videos on requesting an interpreter, how and where to access the public video phone, how to obtain an Access Pass, and driving in the park. In addition, **for visitors with hearing loss**, Yosemite NP has assistive-listening devices in Yosemite Valley Visitor Center for ranger-led programs, public events, and tours in Yosemite Valley, Wawona, Glacier Point, and Tuolumne Meadows. Concessioner lodges also have assistive-listening devices that can be booked in advance (phone: 209-372-1240). Finally, for **visitors with sight loss**, there is an audio description of the park brochure on the UniDescription app, which is available for iOS and Android devices.

ZION, UTAH

Address: Zion National Park, 1 Zion Park Boulevard, State Route 9, Springdale, UT 84767

Phone: 435-772-3256

E-mail: zion_park_information@nps.gov

Website: https://www.nps.gov/zion/index.htm

Accessibility website: https://www.nps.gov/zion/planyourvisit/accessibility.htm

---

Utah

Verbal Image

Utah, known as the Beehive State, is culturally and geographically unique. It is a medium-sized, regular-shaped state on the map and has a population of around 3,200,000 people. Space-wise, Utah is over 350 miles (around 560 kilometers) north to south at its tallest and around 270 miles (around 435 kilometers) east to west at its widest, with over 82,100 square miles (almost 220,000 square kilometers) of land in between. It is a landlocked, almost rectangular state, with highly regular, right-angled borders and major land boundaries with Colorado to the east, Nevada to the west, Arizona to the south, and Idaho and Wyoming to the north. The southeastern point of the state also touches the northwesternmost point of New Mexico's border.[1]

Utah is largely wild country with mountains, deserts, and inland water. However, it also has interesting farmland and produces a broad range of food on more than eighteen thousand farms totaling around eleven million developed acres, and as you'd expect, there are many large-sized farms and much ranch land. Utah is mostly known for rearing cattle, sheep, mink, and pigs; for growing fruits such as cherries and apricots; and for harvesting grains, which are used to feed the local animals. Given the state's nickname, it is also known for its apiary culture. However, beyond this agricultural land lie large areas of unpopulated territory that are controlled by nature, with a vast range of unique flora and fauna.

Utah's landscape is dominated by a number of mountain ranges, such as the traditionally titled Wah Wah, Wasatch, and Black mountain ranges, many of which bisect its central regions and straddle large parts of its borderland. In addition, Utah has what can be described as two types of desert: traditional sand and rock, including the famous Mojave Desert, and salt flats, including the almost legendary Bonneville Salt Flats that gave their name to the Triumph Bonneville motorcycle.

Importantly, given the rain and snow on these mountain ranges, Utah is almost defined by its water, either its running water or its greater lakes. Most importantly, its highly unusual inland Great Salt Lake has a surface area of around one million acres. To put this in context, only Lake Michigan has a larger surface area in the US. Utah is also home to the Colorado River—which, despite its name, is Utah's longest river and flows literally thousands of miles through its landmass—as well as the Bear, Green, and San Juan Rivers.

As for its human culture, Utah was previously a part of Mexico, officially became a part of the US in the late 1840s, and was named a state in the late 1890s. The capital of Utah and by far its largest city is the famous and historical Salt Lake City, which was founded by a group of settlers led by Brigham Young in the late 1840s. Salt Lake City is also important religiously, of course, and it is perhaps best known as the home of the Church of the Latter-day Saints, which is otherwise known as the Mormon faith. The old city itself is home to the central religious complex of the Mormons, which includes a cavernous tabernacle and a library with birth records dating back generations.

As much of Utah's land is mountainous, salt flat, and traditional desert, it is sparsely populated, with the majority of its population living in its large and rapidly growing urban areas. Salt Lake City is north of the center of Utah and is approximately halfway between the state's eastern and western borders. To demonstrate the human emptiness of its interior, a large part of the population of Utah lives in and around Salt Lake City.

It is true that the city limits of Salt Lake City have a current population of only a little over 200,500 people; however, this population rises to almost 1,170,000 people in its metropolitan area, stretching out from its waterfront. To put it another way, almost a third of Utah's population is in this metropolitan area, and it is becoming more so each year, with the metropolitan area growing around 1 percent annually.

Importantly, given that most of Utah's population also lives within fifteen miles of mountain ranges, the state is particularly known for mountain activities and for its winter sports. Perhaps most famously, Salt Lake City hosted the 2002 Winter Olympics both in the city and in its neighboring mountains, and all these Olympic sites are still open to the public for sport.

Climate and Wildlife

Utah's diverse geography, with mountains and deserts and everything in between, means it has largely changeable weather, and on average it has 125 clear days of sunshine a year. Temperature-wise, it can have an average temperature of just under 50 F (just under 10 C), an average summer temperature of just under 70 F (just over 20 C), and its winters have average temperatures over 2 F (just under −2 C). These averages only tell a partial story, though, as its record temperatures show two utter extremes of heat and cold. Consequently, its hottest day on record was an oven-like 115 F (just over 46 C) in the summer of 1985 in the town of St. George, and this contrasts with a deep freeze of around −69 F (around −56 C) in the winter of 1985 at Peter's Sink, although we should note that this frozen temperature was recorded at over eight thousand feet up in the mountains, where weather is almost always extreme.[2]

Similarly, Utah's precipitation is also remarkable. Bearing in mind its mountain ranges, it has snowfall on average almost thirty-five days of the year, and this measures just over 56 inches during an average per year (this is just over 1,420 millimeters). Similarly, the state's current average annual rainfall is just over 12 inches (around 310 millimeters), making it a fairly wet region.

Like its weather, Utah's wildlife is also diverse, and, although not as extreme, there are similarities between it and Alaska. Utah's most famous animals include archetypal predators such as coyotes, black bears, bats, and foxes; the industrious beaver; porcupines; and hunted animals such as chipmunks, deer, the almost iconic bighorn sheep, elk, and rabbits.

Similarly, Utah also has an impressive range of plants, flowers, and trees, such as sunflower, lupine, the relatively local Aspen daisy, buckwheat, flax, and wild geranium. It also has a wide range of trees and bushes such as fir, dogwood, mesquite, oak, acacia, maple, alder, birch, desert willow, juniper, spruce, pine, cottonwood, hawthorn, mountain mahogany, fernbrush, winterfat, and ash. Utah also has many beautifully named rare plants and trees that are worth mentioning, such as velvet ash, indigo bush, rabbitbrush, Mormon Tea, velvet snowbrush ceanothus, bee balm, Rocky Mountain penstemon, Utah serviceberry, four o'clock, Apache plume, and chokecherry.

Zion National Park

Verbal Image

Although it is very much a part of Utah, Zion National Park[3] (Zion NP) is closer to Las Vegas, which is around 160 miles southeast by road, than it is to Salt Lake City, which is over 300 miles to the north. It is also over 380 miles from Phoenix and Los Angeles, which although far away can be reached by automobile in a day or two. The closest main city to Zion is Cedar City, which is just under sixty miles away. The park is also very well visited, and its park shuttle bus (which I write about more below) carried more than six million visitors in 2017, when the last major survey of its transportation was held.

Inside, Zion NP is more than 145,500 acres (or more than 230 square miles) of mountainous and plateaued wilderness with woodland of pine and juniper, spectacular gorges, and cliffs reaching up to 2,000 feet tall. These tallest features frame waterfalls, suspended foliage canyons, and narrow paths that drop into the Mojave Desert.

Its highest peak is Horse Ranch Mountain, which is over 8,700 feet tall, while its lowest peak is Pa'rus Wash, which is a little under 3,700 feet tall. All these spectacular rock formations are the result of a combination of searing heat, freezing temperatures, and water currents from rivers and lakes that are a part of the park's natural history. Consequently, these mountainous and plateauing features give Zion a distinct terrain, with views of unforgettable mesas, rivers, vast rock outcrops rising straight from the earth, and arches carved from desert-heat erosion as well as snow, ice, and flowing water.

Zion National Park is in the extreme southwest of Utah, not far from the border with Arizona, and can be seen in two parts. These two parts of the park are connected by a narrow vertical strip to the north of Zion and based in the well-named Iron County, Kane County, and most of all Washington County. The largest part of Zion is its southeastern sector, which features the wonderful and dangerously named Hurricane Mesa, Zion Canyon, and the park's main visitor center, the latter of which is in the far southern tip of the park. From above, the shape of both parts of the national park are roughly rectangular, with the larger part to the south being tall. Most of the borders are also geometric and set at right angles, but there are some ragged borders where Zion follows the natural path of its flowing canyons and mountains, many of which rise almost vertically.

Zion is designated as Utah's oldest national park and is home to many unique species of mammals, birds, reptiles, amphibians, and fish. The smaller sector of Zion that is set apart from its major lands features the beautiful Kolob Canyons and is to the west of Kolob reservoir; this reservoir is not a part of the park though.

Getting Around Zion

At present, Zion has a number of accessible facilities for **visitors with access needs**; a brief overview of these at the time of writing is as follows:

- "During COVID. . . . The park is currently allowing visitors that use wheelchairs to get a special pass from the Visitor Center to drive up canyon. [Before COVID] the shuttle bus was accessible to all but the largest motorized wheelchairs, and it served as the main 'tour' of the Park. So the focus has been on making all the experiences we could accessible for as many visitors as possible, rather than creating a separate experience. An audio tour for those driving up-canyon on their own is available online [through, for example, the] Shuttle Narration—Zion National Park. [There is more on this below.]

- Ride with a Ranger. . . . This program, prior to COVID, was conducted daily from Memorial Day until September 29 and started at the Zion Canyon Visitor Center. This program will be back once we resume our Ranger programming. These tours last two hours. Seats are limited [but you can] make free reservations, in person, up to three days in advance at the information desk at the Zion Canyon Visitor Center. No telephone reservations are accepted. Note: Because large groups can impact the availability of seats for other visitors, a group size is limited to 8. This includes people sharing the same affiliation (school, club, scout troop, family, friends) on any one tour.

- Concession horse ride—we currently have a transfer station at the Zion Lodge for visitors who use a wheelchair who are physically able to maintain their torso in an upright position [and] can do the trail ride. Zion also has an additional transfer station [that] will be install[ed] at Hop Valley in the future."

As with many national parks nowadays, there is a shuttle bus route that will take you around Zion NP and that has been running since the beginning of the millennium. In the park, and with only a few exceptions, you can usually only travel through Zion Canyon by the park's shuttle bus throughout spring, summer, and fall. Zion NP places great emphasis on using this bus, as it is trying to reduce traffic and pollution and provide a pleasant experience for all its visitors. These buses are largely accessible for visitors with mobility access issues, can accommodate wheelchairs, and generally have mobility lifts for entry, although there are some restrictions to the wheelchairs it can normally handle—you can find more information on these restrictions via its accessibility web page. "The shuttle ride up the Scenic Drive is a wonderful way to see or hear about the highlights of Zion. It is free with the park entrance and is accessible to wheelchair users with a combined weight of less than 600 lbs and smaller than 45" long or 25" wide. The shuttle itself has a kneeling function to make stepping up into it easier, or an integrated lift can be utilized by the shuttle driver. . . . Currently during COVID this does not apply. All wheelchair users can receive a pass and drive-up canyon."

As with a number of other national parks, such as Denali, you can only travel through the park in your own or a supporter's automobile if you have medical equipment or it is dangerous for you to be on public transport.[4] Permits for using private automobiles can be granted on request by the park, and I would strongly advise asking about these permits at least a month before you visit the park. Once in Zion NP, you can get the permit from the Zion Valley Visitor Center information desk (phone: 435-772-3256).

There are two shuttle routes: inside the park and outside the park. For the bus inside the park, you'll need to pay in advance through the general federal government website: https://www.rec reation.gov. This internal bus takes what is called a circulator route and travels down Scenic Drive up and through the southern section of the park and outward. Outside the park, the shuttle bus has no fare and can be picked up in the nearby settlement of Springdale, which is not too far from the park's entrance. Throughout the summer, these outside buses run regularly on a loop from early in the morning until late evening. For **visitors with vision loss** or other **visitors with access needs** who find visiting the park too difficult, a shuttle audio description is available: https://www.nps.gov/zion/ learn/photosmultimedia/shuttle-narration.htm. For more information on the shuttle bus, to download the audio description, or to look up times, stops, and facilities at Zion Canyon, phone 435-772-3256.

If you have a permit for an automobile to travel through Zion NP, you'll need to be aware that there is only a single park road, and sites along the way are likely to have few parking spaces that cannot be guaranteed. This said, the parking spaces that are available are relatively accessible, even though they are often not designated access spaces.

For walkers and riders, Zion NP has extensive information on its main trails that you can study before you visit, which lets you decide whether you want to approach the trail or not. Importantly, Zion NP has a number of mountainous trails that can be accessed from its main centers, lodges, and campgrounds, some of which are accessible for **people with mobility access needs**.

For example, at the time of writing, one of the most accessible trails is the Pa'rus Trail, which is around a mile and a half long and can be used by different modes of transport. The trail itself is largely paved or covered with either tar or concrete; however, it should be noted that even this trail can be damaged by cold weather, so it is best to check with the park how easy these surfaces are if you have mobility issues. Pa'rus Trail is also easy to get to as it is close to Zion Canyon Visitor Center, where it is largely unsloping and can often be used by wheeling if needed. However, where it goes forward toward the South Campground, it can get steeper, so you'll need to take this into account.

> The Pa'rus Trail (as accessed from the Nature Center Overflow parking area) is the premier accessible trail in the Park. Wayside exhibits are currently under development to provide a more universally meaningful experience, and the trail itself is fully paved. Visitors can typically access the Zion Transportation System at Canyon Junction or make it an in-and-out trail. It is 1.5 miles long and 8–10' wide. The majority of the path has between a 2% and 5% running slope, although three short sections have slopes up to 9%. The trail is exposed to direct sunlight, but there are shade structures and some trees in spots.

More specialist transport in the park includes horseback riding and "canyoneering," which can be booked via private concessioners and includes tours. As these forms of travel are booked through external concessioners, they won't be covered in this book.

Zion's Facilities
Zion has been actively developing access for several decades, in particular:

- "At Zion National Park, especially since 2000, with the construction of the new Visitor Center & transportation system, all of the Park's new facilities and major renovations have been constructed with physical accessibility in mind. 2000 was a turning point of planning for accessibility.

- Our Superintendent has been involved in national planning and was instrumental in the NPS 2015 5-year Accessibility Strategic Plan, All In! to improve its approach to making national parks more accessible and enjoyable for those with disabilities and their families. The plan encompasses a 3-tiered goal approach.

- Zion [hosted] an expo style event for staff that [included] training on awareness of disabilities. This [provided] staff an opportunity to learn best practices and how to provide better customer service for a variety of visitors. These expos were hosted annually from 2013–2017."

In comparison to other national parks, Zion NP has relatively few visitor centers; however, the centers and the other learning, leisure, and information spaces that exist are extensive and have generally accessible facilities. These centers have varying opening hours dependent on the seasons and weather conditions, with the longest hours being in the summer and the shortest hours being in the winter. There are also some periods where the centers, like the park's roads and other facilities, may be closed altogether because of extreme climatic conditions or natural events such as earthquakes.

These centers include **Zion Canyon Visitor Center**, which is just inside Zion National Park (1 Zion Park Boulevard, Springdale UT 84767, phone: 435-772-3256). This center is closest to the southernmost entrance to the park, less than a quarter mile or so (around half a kilometer), so it is usually the first point of contact for many visitors. As I wrote above, it is also a changeover point for the shuttle bus route. The park's orientation video, which shows in the center, has closed captions for **visitors with hearing loss**, and for **visitors with sight loss**, there is a video that is audio described. I would advise contacting the center before you visit for more details about what is available.

For **visitors with mobility access needs**, the center has largely accessible restrooms, some accessible parking spaces although these can't be guaranteed, and largely accessible walkways from the parking lot to the building. For **visitors who use wheelchairs**, the information desk and water fountain are wheelchair-user height. Outside the visitor center, a picnic area by the parking lot also has a restroom, eating spaces, and tables that are largely accessible.

In the far northwest of the park, **Kolob Canyons Visitor Center** is just off the Veterans Memorial Highway (3752 E Kolob Canyon Road, New Harmony, UT 84757, phone: 435-586-9548). The visitor center is a part of the Zion National Park Forever Project (https://zionpark.org/events/) and has a bookstore and a desk for paying the park's entrance fees and applying for or collecting permits. This includes the permits you'll need to use a private automobile in the park if you have additional medical needs that prevent you from riding the bus farther into Zion NP. As with the main visitor center, the Kolob center also has a nearby picnic area, although this has varying access for **people with mobility access needs** and fewer facilities. As with the Zion Canyon Visitor Center, the orientation film has closed captions for **visitors with hearing loss**.

Around Zion Creek is also **Zion Human History Museum** (Zion National Park Road, Springdale, UT 84767, phone: 435-772-3256 or e-mail: zion_museum@nps.gov). This is a museum of the anthropology of southern Utah and focuses on American Indian culture. In addition, the museum also has exhibits about the settlement of Utah by those who followed Brigham Young from the eastern states in the early days of the Union and the settlement of the area that is now Zion NP itself. For **visitors with hearing loss**, the museum has a largely accessible video on the background to the park. For **visitors with mobility access needs**, the outside of the building has a ramp running up to the entrance and largely accessible parking spaces, largely accessible bathrooms, and water-filling stations.

In the same area of the park, **Grotto Picnic Area**, which is just off the Zion Canyon Scenic Drive, is largely accessible to **visitors with mobility access needs** with level, compacted-gravel surface picnic spaces and paths around. The grounds also have a largely accessible bathroom. However, you should note that, generally speaking, the picnic area can only be used from spring through fall inclusive and has a stop for the shuttle bus, although for visitors with special permissions, there are regular parking spaces available during spring, summer, and fall.

If you need medical assistance in the park or you need permanent medical support, the following are medical centers or places that can be reached or that can provide remote treatment:

- **Zion Canyon Medical Clinic** at 120 Lion Boulevard, Springdale, UT 84767. Phone: 435-772-3226.

- **Hurricane Valley Clinic (Intermountain Healthcare)** at 75 N 2260 W, Hurricane, UT 84737. Phone: 435-635-6500.

- **Indie Med** at 25 2000 W #3, Hurricane, UT 84737. Phone: 435-635-1148.

- **Kane County Hospital** at 355 Main Street, Kanab, UT 84741. Phone: 435-644-5811.

- **Family Healthcare St. George Medical Clinic** at 25 North 100 East Suite 102, St. George, Utah 84770. Phone: 435-986-2565

- **Coral Canyon Joint and Spine Health** at 83 S 2600 W #102, Hurricane, UT 84737. Phone: 435-635-7771.

- **Creek Valley Health Clinic** at 20 S Colvin Street, Colorado City, AZ 86021. Phone: 435-900-1104.

Lodges and Campgrounds

Because its temperatures can be extreme in different seasons, especially in its gorges and around and atop its mountain ranges, **Zion Lodge** in Zion Canyon can be a safe choice for those with a number of access needs. Generally speaking, you can only reach the lodge by shuttle bus unless you have a permit because of your access needs in all but winter; however, for those with permits, there are accessible parking spaces and a ramp outside for **visitors with mobility access needs**.

In addition, the lodge's auditorium, eating areas, shop, and bathrooms are said to be largely accessible for those with **mobility access needs**, and the auditorium offers largely accessible events such as lectures arranged by the park. The lodge also has a small number of rooms that comply with the ADA, although these are limited, so I would strongly advise you to get in touch with the lodge to book these rooms at least three months before you plan to visit Zion NP (again, this is still not guaranteed).

The Lava Point Campground is high up in the mountains and opens throughout the spring and summer months and has perhaps the most basic facilities of all the campgrounds in the park, including the most basic toilet facilities and no running water. It is important to note, however, that it can close in bad weather and can only be visited in regular-sized or small automobiles.

The Watchman Campground is just off the main Zion Canyon Visitor Center and has developed facilities and areas for people with access needs both visiting as groups, in families, or on their own. Although it is surrounded by sloping grounds, it is near the visitor center and can be reached by the shuttle bus or private automobiles. The campsite can also be accessed via a pathway with a hard surface and is close to an open-air amphitheater with accessible seating, where talks are given about the park.

A little less than half a mile from the Watchman Campground and along Zion Mount Carmel Highway, the park's **South Campground** has no accessible bathrooms or showers but has flat areas for pitching tents. However, being just a little farther into the park, this campground has more open scenery and is next to open water.

Learning Programs and Tours

As with other similar parks, Zion NP offers ranger-led talks and tours, field classes, and lectures from spring through fall, which are most often based in the area around the Zion Canyon Visitor Center and the campgrounds close by. Information about these lectures and ranger-led programs are advertised in the visitor centers, in the park newspaper (https://www.nps.gov/zion/learn/news/newspaper .htm), on the Zion NP website, and on the Zion National Park Forever Project website (https://zionpark.org/).[5] You can also see which tours are accessible for **visitors with mobility access needs** in the park newspaper, as accessible tours are advertised with relevant symbols.

Visitors with hearing loss can borrow assisted-listening devices for the ranger-led tours from the Zion Human History Museum, although you will need to book these devices in advance. In addition, under more normal circumstances, Zion NP can also arrange an ASL translator, although at the time of writing, this service had been suspended because of COVID-19 restrictions. If you want to arrange for an assisted-listening device, I advise contacting the park at least a week before you plan to attend your tour, and when sign language translators are available again, I would advise contacting the service at least two months in advance to arrange a signer (e-mail: zion_park_information@nps.gov or phone: 435-772-3256). Assistive-listening devices are available by reservation for all ranger-led programs. The museum also organizes what are termed patio talks not far outside its building, which are accessible for **visitors with mobility access needs.**

There are a number of guided and nonguided walks designed for **visitors with mobility access needs,** although you'll need to be aware that you should bring water and that there are generally no accessible bathrooms along the way. Walks that were advertised by Zion NP at the time of writing included Pa'rus Trail, an approximately two-mile hike from Canyon Junction to the Zion Canyon Visitor Center; ranger-guided hikes, including a one-and-three-quarter-mile guided walk on the Pa'rus Trail, which goes from the Virgin River to Canyon Junction; and Ride with a Ranger, a two-hour commented tour in the Zion Canyon, which runs from Zion Canyon Visitor Center. Zion NP warn visitors that this tour fills up quickly and that it can be booked by visitors with access issues up to three days in advance (phone: 435-772-3256). The Watchman Campsite runs a largely accessible evening program of lectures on various themes connected to the park, such as its wildlife and human cultures, in its amphitheater. The amphitheater, as I wrote above, is largely accessible to **people with mobility access needs** and has largely accessible bathrooms and parking spaces in its lot nearby.

Featured Online Learning

Zion NP has walking tours presented as time-lapsed videos for those who cannot make it to the park, including **visitors with severe mobility access needs** or those who want to plan visits before arriving. Some of the video descriptions also talk about the accessibility of the tours. Most of these videos have no audio, and none of the videos have closed captions or audio description; however, there are detailed, typed descriptions of each of their tours. In other instances, videos may have wildlife noises but no commentary.[6]

In addition to these virtual tours and hikes, you can also listen to the shuttle bus narrative, the one played as you enter and tour the park, from its website. The narrative is accessible to **visitors with hearing loss** and **visitors with sight loss,** as it can be listened to through a streamed or downloadable MP3 file, the latter of which can be listened to off-line, or can be accessed as a script that can be downloaded or printed and brought to the park to read as you tour (https://www.nps.gov/zion/learn/photosmultimedia/shuttle -narration.htm).

The tour itself includes the actual timing of the tour that you will be able to take in the park, including the gaps in speech and what lies outside the bus, to the left and right. Part of the tour includes narratives by people connected with the park, such as a local American Indian person whose ancestors first settled the area of the park, and a professional photographer.

Beyond its website, there is also a downloadable Tour of Zion app. The app is a more accessible platform on which you can see photographs and maps of the area, watch tour videos, and see scanned 3-D representations of the land. You can also get road directions for particular views in the park and Zion-Mount Carmel Highway, times and routes of buses and railroads, the history of the area, and the history of Zion NP. The app is available for Apple's iOS and Android mobile devices from their respective download stores.

In addition, Zion runs social media accounts, including Twitter, Facebook, and Instagram. And, as they told me, "we follow best practices for making these published posts to be inclusive."

Specialized Access

At present, Zion is developing a number of accessible initiatives. These include:

- "[The park is undergoing, a form of self-evaluation of all its services and facilities know as] Accessibility Compliance: This involves helping all visitors have a positive and rewarding experience at our venues.

- [The park is] currently finalizing the Zion Accessibility Guide to provide a comprehensive source for accessibility information for visitors.

- [The park has] Braille information booklets available.

- [The park has a] newly published Historic Driving Tour brochure. This provides historic photos and information of the scenic drive through Zion National Park.

- Zion staff are also working with region to do a large format unigrid for Zion National Park."

Finally, and back at its website, Zion NP has an accessibility self-evaluation document that can be downloaded from its accessibility web page. The document was originally developed close to the beginning of the five-year plan that I described earlier in this book. From there, it was decided to make it available to all **visitors with access needs** to help plan their own journey and publicize the facilities and services available (https://www.nps.gov/zion/learn/management/upload/ZION-SE-Appendix-A-10-28-16.pdf). You should note, however, that the document is a PDF, so some **visitors with sight loss** may find it difficult to access the text with traditional screen readers.

In addition, and as with its transport plans and facilities, Zion works with volunteers and contractors to accessibly support learning for **visitors with hearing loss**. This includes:

- "The park is currently partnering with Dixie State University (DSU) to provide ASL signers when requested . . . [and] working in partnership with the DSU to do ASL interpreted Park videos that will be available online.

- Zion is currently a part of a community of practice around Deaf Resources. The goal of this group is to provide best practices, training, and facilitate better visitor experiences at National Parks.

- In the region, there are ASL youth crews and Zion is working to potentially host a crew in the future."

NOTES

Preface

1. John M. Kennedy and Igor Juricevic, "Foreshortening, Convergence and Drawings from a Blind Adult," *Perception* 35, no. 6 (2006): 847–51; Simon Hayhoe, Ruby Cohen, and Helena Garcia-Carrisoza, "Locke and Hume's Theory of Color Is Interrogated through a Case Study of Esref Armagan, an Artist Born Blind," *Journal of Blindness Innovation and Research* 9, no. 1 (2019): 1.

Introduction

1. Santoshi Halder and Vassilios Argyropoulos, *Inclusion, Equity, and Access for Individuals with Disabilities* (Singapore: Springer, 2019), 257.

Chapter One

1. Personal communication with Alfred, National Parks Service Headquarters, 2018.
2. Simon Hayhoe, *Cultural Heritage, Ageing, Disability, and Identity: Practice, and the Development of Inclusive Capital* (New York: Routledge, 2019).
3. Ibid.

4. National Parks Service, *The National Parks Service Special Directive 83-3* (Washington, DC: National Parks Service, 1983).

5. Simon Hayhoe, *Philosophy as Disability and Exclusion: The Development of Theories on Blindness, Touch, and the Arts in England, 1688–2010* (Charlotte, NC: Information Age Publishing, 2016).

6. National Parks Service. *Director's Order #42* (Washington, DC: National Parks Service, 2000).

7. Ibid.

8. National Parks Service. *Director's Order 16A* (Washington, DC: National Parks Service, 1999).

9. 1. Associate Director, Park Operations and Education, is primarily responsible for and guides access throughout the NPS system.

(a) Park Facility Management Division—Looks after maintenance at all facilities and has responsibility for making sure parks comply with architectural accessibility legislation.

(b) Interpretation and Education Division—Developed and made sure of the legal compliance of educational programs, park tours, and other visitor learning—including online—in parks nationwide.

(c) Concession Management Division—Simply has responsibility for permissions and the running of concessions stands and outlets through the parks system.

(d) Harpers Ferry Center—is the center that designs and implements all forms of accessible technologies and media in national parks nationwide.

2. Associate Director, Professional Services oversees the design, planning, and implementation of construction, servicing, and alterations of buildings and sites nationwide.

(a) Park Planning and Special Studies—Planned all aspects of policy as it related to the buildings and services provided by NPS nationwide.

(b) Denver Service Center (DSC)—the DSC designed and planned new buildings and sites and renovated existing buildings where it was needed.

3. Associate Director, Administration, which had responsibility for looking after and providing support for staff and for making sure that NPS complied with laws and regulations relating to workers' rights.

(a) Office of Human Resources—was responsible for fair standards of recruitment, hiring, promotions, and so forth and compliance with the law and "reasonable accommodations."

(b) Training and Development Division—which had responsibility for training at a local, regional, and national level and that training was in compliance with the regulations.

4. Equal Opportunity Program, which made sure legally mandated civil rights were being complied with as a part of the Department of the Interior Equal Opportunity Program.

10. Laws, regulations, and standards set out in the Director's Orders:

Laws:

1. The Architectural Barriers Act of 1968 (P.L. 90-480) "requires all buildings and facilities built or renovated in whole or in part with Federal funds to be accessible to, and usable by, physically disabled persons."

2. Section 504 of the Rehabilitation Act of 1973 (P.L. 93-112) "requires program accessibility in all [Government] services."

3. Section 501 of the Rehabilitation Act of 1973, as amended, "prohibits discrimination against people with disabilities in all employment practices within the Federal Government."

4. Section 508 of the Rehabilitation Act of 1973, as amended, "requires that all Federal agencies ensure that when they develop, procure, maintain, or use electronic and information technology; that, it is accessible to employees with disabilities."

5. Americans with Disabilities Act of 1990.

Regulations:

1. Enforcement of Nondiscrimination on the Basis of Handicap in Department of the Interior Programs (43 CFR 17.501-17.570). "[Operate] all its programs and activities to ensure nondiscrimination against qualified persons with a disability."

Standards:

1. Uniform Federal Accessibility Standards (UFAS). "This document presents uniform standards for the design, construction, and alteration of buildings so that individuals with disabilities will have ready access to and use of them in accord with the Architectural Barriers Act of 1968."

2. Americans with Disabilities Act Accessibility Guidelines (ADAAG).

11. National Parks Service, *All In! Accessibility in the National Park Service, Five-Year Strategic Plan* (Washington, DC: National Parks Service, 2015).

12. Personal communication with Alfred, National Parks Service Headquarters, 2018.

13. According to the 2015 strategic plan, the app was originally designed only to be used outdoors. However, during its development, iBeacons, then a new technology, were released for the first time, and this allowed the NPS to conduct a pilot trial of the app indoors to provide audio description whenever visitors moved close to exhibits with an iBeacon attached.

14. These departments included the Parks Facilities Management Division; the National Accessibility Branch; Park Planning, Facilities, and Lands; and Interpretation and Education.

15. This included the Office of Personnel Management and the Federal Working Group on Executive Order 13548, including the Office of Disability Employment Policy at the Department of Labor and Federal Partners in Transition—the latter was a federal coalition that lobbied for employment opportunities for people with disabilities.

16. This committee was renamed the Service-wide Accessibility Coordinating Committee (SWACC) in the plan.

17. The culmination of this activity meant that a group titled the Development Advisory Board (DAB) was redesigned to focus on projects reviewed by the board's staff, with changes being made to programs and projects that did not meet the guidelines they set. In addition to these ongoing evaluations, numerous research and experimental evaluation task forces were introduced.

For instance, a temporary working group of regional experts that could research less accessible projects that had not long finished was formed. This group's sole task was to examine broader issues that had arisen in parks that, it was felt, needed to be avoided again and report back on how this information could be used for better providing access across the regions. In addition, as part of this ongoing effort, HFC undertook a broad data collection exercise in order to provide a more targeted approach to identifying the parks' most practical access needs. This was to allow a more targeted approach to providing access and resourcing this access as the five-year plan unfolded.

Other targeted practical initiatives by HFC that were reported in 2015 include (1) seventy new Braille titles by HFC Publications and an HFC Braille Publication Guide (see the website http://www.nps.gov/hfc/accessibility/brailleGuide.cfm) in early summer 2015; (2) the center purchased almost 130 portable assistive-listening kits, half of which were distributed throughout the nation's parks; (3) a new FAQs section and an accessible PDF brochure became a permanent feature on HFC's accessibility web page (http://www.nps.gov/hfc/accessibility/); (4) online training on access for visitors with hearing loss (https://www.doi.gov/doilearn); (5) IMR (Intermountain Region, comprising Wyoming, Utah, Texas, Oklahoma, New Mexico, Montana, Colorado, and Arizona) worked on providing a number of large-print, audio, and Braille versions of brochures, although this initiative did not appear to be completed during the 2015 reporting period.

18. These events included the Arts-n-Recreation ADA network webinar and the 2015 LEAD conference.

19. Eleven parks were part of a pilot project conducted by the Pacific West Region.

20. The AXS branch, DSC, NCA, HFC.

21. As Alfred explained, "The National Accessibility Branch is within the Parks Facilities Management Division, under the Associate Director for Parks Planning, Facilities, and Land. The National Accessibility Branch has a Branch Chief and two accessibility specialists. This team of three then collaborates with 7 part-time Regional Accessibility Coordinators, though the Regional Coordinators do not report to or work for the National Accessibility Branch. In turn, the 7 Regional Coordinators collaborate with the part-time accessibility coordinators at each park, though the park coordinators do not report to the Regional Coordinators. The National Accessibility Branch also collaborates with others across the service, such as the specialist on accessible media and exhibits."

22. Personal communication with Alfred, National Parks Service Headquarters, 2018.

23. Personal communication with Alfred, National Parks Service Headquarters, 2018.

Chapter Two

1. National Parks Service. *Director's Order #42* (Washington, DC: National Parks Service, 2000).

2. Paul Saettler, *A History of Instructional Technology* (New York: McGraw-Hill, 1968).

3. Roger Reiser and John Dempsey, *Trends and Issues in Instructional Design and Technology* (London: Pearson, 2011).

4. Ivan Pavlov, *Conditioned Reflexes* (Mineola, NY: Dover Publications, 1927).

5. Edward Thorndike, "Animal Intelligence: An Experimental Study of the Associative Processes in Animals," *Psychological Monographs: General and Applied* 2, no. 4 (1898): i–109.

6. Buhurus Skinner, *Beyond Freedom and Dignity* (New York: Bantam Books, 1972).

7. Ibid.

8. Reiser and Dempsey, *Trends and Issues.*

9. Simon Hayhoe, *Philosophy as Disability and Exclusion: The Development of Theories on Blindness, Touch, and the Arts in England, 1688–2010* (Charlotte, NC: Information Age Publishing, 2016).

10. Ibid.

11. United Nations, *Enable: Rights and Dignity of Persons with Disability* (Geneva, Switzerland: United Nations, 2006).

12. Architectural and Transportation Barriers Compliance Board, "Electronic and Information Technology Accessibility Standards (36 CFR Part 1194)," *Federal Register* 65, no. 246 (2000): 80500–28.

13. Simon Hayhoe, "Epistemological Trends in the Literature on Mobile Devices, Mobile Learning, and Learners with Visual Impairments," *Optometry and Vision Science* 95, no. 9 (2018): 889–97.

14. John Clarkson, Paul Langdon, and Peter Robinson, *Designing Accessible Technology* (London: Springer, 2006).

15. Simon Hayhoe, "An Enquiry into Passive and Active Exclusion from Unreachable Artworks in the Museum: Two Case Studies of Final-Year Students at California School for the Blind Studying Artworks through Galleries and on the Web," *British Journal of Visual Impairment* 32, no. 1 (2014): 44–58.

16. National Parks Service, *Director's Order #42.*

Chapter Three

1. "About Maine," State of Maine, accessed December 25, 2020, https://www.maine.gov/portal/about_me/index.html.
2. "The Climate of Maine," Weather Atlas, accessed December 25, 2020, https://www.weather-us.com/en/maine-usa-climate#climate_text_1.
3. All of the following facts, facilities, and services were checked on "Acadia National Park, Maine," National Parks Service, accessed December 25, 2020, https://www.nps.gov/acad/index.htm.
4. Douglas Deur, *The Park Lands of Isle au Haut: A Community Oral History* (Seattle: University of Washington, 2013).

Chapter Four

1. "Alaska Information," State of Alaska, accessed December 25, 2020, http://alaska.gov/kids/learn/information.htm.
2. "The Climate of Alaska," Weather Atlas, accessed December 25, 2020, https://www.weather-us.com/en/Alaska-usa-climate#climate_text_1.
3. All of the following facts, facilities, and services were checked on "Denali National Park, Alaska," National Parks Service, accessed December 25, 2020, https://www.nps.gov/dena/index.htm.

Chapter Five

1. "Weird, Wonderful Facts about Florida," Visit Florida, accessed December 25, 2020, https://www.visitflorida.com/en-us/travel-ideas/10-florida-facts.html.
2. "The Climate of Florida," Weather Atlas, accessed December 25, 2020, https://www.weather-us.com/en/florida-usa-climate#climate_text_1.
3. All of the following facts, facilities and services were checked on "Everglades National Park, Florida," National Parks Service, accessed December 25, 2020, https://www.nps.gov/ever/index.htm.
4. "Everglades National Park," UNESCO, accessed December 25, 2020, https://whc.unesco.org/en/list/76/.
5. At the time of writing, these materials and lesson plans included the following examples: a Wilderness Fact Sheet, Marjory Stoneman Douglas Wilderness Laws, a Wilderness Trip Planner, maps of the protected

areas in the park, an Everglades ID Sheet, a South Florida National Parks Activity Guide, Climate Change Activities, and Everglades Mountains and Valleys Lesson Plans.

Chapter Six

1. "Pennsylvania Facts & History," VisitPA, accessed December 25, 2020, https://www.visitpa.com/facts-and-history.

2. "The Climate of Pennsylvania," Weather Atlas, accessed December 25, 2020, https://www.weather-us.com/en/pennsylvania-usa-climate#climate_text_1.

3. All of the following facts, facilities, and services were checked on: "Gettysburg National Military Park, Pennsylvania," National Parks Service, accessed December 25, 2020, https://www.nps.gov/gett/index.htm.

4. At the time of writing, the following were offered as choices for the tour: For elementary students, the "Flat Ranger's Rock Tour" asked, "Which battlefield rock/monument story is your favorite?" The "Flat Ranger's Time Travel" tour asked the question, "How do old buildings help us understand the perspectives of those who used them?" For elementary and lower-middle-school students, the "Re-enlist?" tour asked the question, "After having served in a Civil War army for three months, would you decide to re-enlist to serve for three years?" For middle and high school students, the "Tide of Battle" tour asked the question, "Which moments were the turning points of the Battle of Gettysburg and of the Civil War?" The "Decision Points" tour asked the question, "What special circumstances did African American residents in Gettysburg face during the campaign and battle, and what were the potential consequences of their decisions?" The "Cost of War?" tour asked the question, "Were the consequences of war, including the destruction and loss of life at Gettysburg, necessary to resolve the country's issues?" For high school students, the "Monumental Issues" tour asked the question, "How can monuments help or hinder a full understanding of American history?" And, lastly, for students of all grades, the "Path of Lincoln" tour asked the question, "How did President Abraham Lincoln's trip to Gettysburg progress the meaning of the Civil War?" and the "Hometown History" tour asked the question, "What are some of *your* family and hometown connections to the American Civil War?"

Chapter Seven

1. "Discover Arizona," State of Arizona, accessed December 25, 2020, https://az.gov/discover.

2. "The Climate of Arizona," Weather Atlas, accessed December 25, 2020, https://www.weather-us.com/en/arizona-usa-climate#climate_text_1.

3. All of the following facts, facilities, and services were checked on "Grand Canyon National Park, Arizona," National Parks Service, accessed December 25, 2020, https://www.nps.gov/grca/index.htm.

4. "Grand Canyon National Park," UNESCO, accessed December 25 2020, https://whc.unesco.org/en/list/75/.

5. It should be emphasized that the park says it can only take wheelchairs less than 30 inches by 48 inches (this is around 76 centimeters by 122 centimeters).

6. Examples of online programs that were advertised at the time of writing included Ask a Ranger, which was offered to school students from third grade through fifth grade; The Human Story, on the communities in the park, which was offered for school students from fourth grade through eighth grade; The Condor's Flight, which was offered to school students from third grade through seventh grade; Ranger Careers, which looks at the job of the ranger around the park and was offered to school students from kindergarten through twelfth grade; and lastly my personal favorite, Sesame Street Explores Grand Canyon, which sort of spoke for itself and was offered for pre-kindergarten students.

Chapter Eight

1. "Washington," Visit USA, accessed December 25, 2020, https://www.visittheusa.co.uk/state/washington.

2. "The Climate of Washington," Weather Atlas, accessed December 25, 2020, https://www.weather-us.com/en/washington-usa-climate#climate_text_1.

3. All of the following facts, facilities, and services were checked on "Olympic National Park, Washington," National Parks Service, accessed December 25, 2020, https://www.nps.gov/olym/index.htm.

4. Example site guides at the time of writing include Mora and Rialto Site Guide (https://www.nps.gov/olym/planyourvisit/mora-area-brochure

.htm) and Kaloch Area Guide (https://www.nps.gov/olym/planyourvisit/kalaloch-area-brochure.htm).

5. Places you could hear about at the time of writing include Elwha, Hurricane Ridge, Lake Crescent, Sol Duc, Mora and Ozette, Hoh, Kalaloch, Quinault, Staircase, and Park Overview.

Chapter Nine

1. "Colorado Facts and History," State of Colorado, accessed December 25, 2020, https://www.colorado.gov/pacific/archives/ColoradoFacts.

2. https://www.colorado.com/articles/colorado-mountains-6-famous-peaks.

3. "The Climate of Colorado," Weather Atlas, accessed December 25, 2020, https://www.weather-us.com/en/colorado-usa-climate#climate_text_1.

4. All of the following facts, facilities, and services were checked on "Rocky Mountain National Park, Colorado," National Parks Service, accessed December 25, 2020, https://www.nps.gov/romo/index.htm.

Chapter Ten

1. "About Wyoming," State of Wyoming, accessed December 25, 2020, http://www.wyo.gov/about-wyoming.

2. "The Climate of Wyoming," Weather Atlas, accessed December 25, 2020, https://www.weather-us.com/en/wyoming-usa-climate#climate_text_1.

3. All of the following facts, facilities, and services were checked on "Yellowstone National Park, Wyoming," National Parks Service, accessed December 25, 2020, https://www.nps.gov/yell/index.htm.

4. Popular accessible parking lots include: Old Faithful Central Parking Lot, which has a large number of spaces, with some for oversized automobiles; Old Faithful Visitor Education Center Parking Lot, which has a number of accessible spaces; Old Faithful East Parking Lot by Old Faithful Inn and the Old Faithful Lodge, which has a number of accessible spaces; South Rim Drive south of Canyon Village, which has a number of accessible spaces; the Boiling River Swim Area west lot, which has a single accessible parking space; and Midway Geyser Basin Parking Lot, which has a number of accessible parking spaces.

5. Examples of the ranger-led programs at the time of writing include Experience Wildlife in Yellowstone; Evening Program around an outside campfire; Gazing into the Abyss, on the hot springs and the geysers in the park; Canyon Talks at Artist Point, on art created in the park; tours including citizen science around the park; and the following walks: Mud Volcano Ramble, Lake Scenic Cruise, Hot Springs Terraces, and Geyser Hill Walk.

Chapter Eleven

1. The city is named after the Sacramento River, on which it lies.

2. "California History Section," State of California Library, accessed December 25, 2020, https://www.library.ca.gov/california-history/.

3. "The Climate of California," Weather Atlas, accessed December 25, 2020, https://www.weather-us.com/en/california-usa-climate#climate_text_1.

4. All of the following facts, facilities, and services were checked on "Yosemite National Park, California," National Parks Service, accessed December 25, 2020, https://www.nps.gov/yose/index.htm.

Chapter Twelve

1. "About Utah," State of Utah, accessed December 25, 2020, https://www.utah.gov/about/.

2. "The Climate of Utah," Weather Atlas, accessed December 25, 2020, https://www.weather-us.com/en/utah-usa-climate#climate_text_1.

3. All of the following facts, facilities, and services were checked on "Zion National Park, Utah," National Parks Service, accessed December 25, 2020, https://www.nps.gov/zion/index.htm.

4. At the time of writing, bus drivers were unfortunately not able to support visitors with wheelchairs on buses. As a consequence, visitors in wheelchairs were normally given a permit to be driven through the park in a private vehicle.

5. These lectures and tours can be studied by young visitors to get a Junior Ranger badge.

6. At the time of writing, these were the advertised walks, although these of course may change with seasons (https://www.nps.gov/zion/learn/photosmultimedia/virtual-hikes.htm): Riverside Walk, a one-mile trek

from Temple of Sinawava to the Narrows, with no commentary; Kayenta Trail, a one-mile trek in Zion Canyon from the Grotto to Heaps Canyon, without commentary; Canyon Overlook Trail, a one-mile trek in Zion Canyon from Zion-Mount Carmel Tunnel to Pine Creek Canyon, without commentary; and Watchman Trail, a three-mile hike from Zion Canyon Visitor Center to up through the canyon, also without commentary.

BIBLIOGRAPHY

Books and Articles

Architectural and Transportation Barriers Compliance Board. "Electronic and Information Technology Accessibility Standards (36 CFR Part 1194)." *Federal Register* 65, no. 246 (2000): 80500–28.

Clarkson, John, Paul Langdon, and Peter Robinson. *Designing Accessible Technology.* London: Springer, 2006.

Deur, Douglas. *The Park Lands of Isle au Haut: A Community Oral History.* Seattle: University of Washington, 2013.

Halder, Santoshi, and Vassilios Argyropoulos. *Inclusion, Equity, and Access for Individuals with Disabilities.* Singapore: Springer, 2019.

Hayhoe, Simon. *Cultural Heritage, Ageing, Disability, and Identity: Practice, and the Development of Inclusive Capital.* New York: Routledge, 2019.

———. "An Enquiry into Passive and Active Exclusion from Unreachable Artworks in the Museum: Two Case Studies of Final-Year Students at California School for the Blind Studying Artworks through Galleries and on the Web." *British Journal of Visual Impairment* 32, no. 1 (2014): 44–58.

———. "Epistemological Trends in the Literature on Mobile Devices, Mobile Learning, and Learners with Visual Impairments." *Optometry and Vision Science* 95, no. 9 (2018): 889–97.

———. *Philosophy as Disability and Exclusion: The Development of Theories on Blindness, Touch, and the Arts in England, 1688–2010.* Charlotte, NC: Information Age Publishing, 2016.

Hayhoe, Simon, Ruby Cohen, and Helena Garcia-Carrisoza. "Locke and Hume's Theory of Color Is Interrogated through a Case Study of Esref Armagan, an Artist Born Blind." *Journal of Blindness Innovation and Research* 9, no. 1 (2019): 1.

Kennedy, John M., and Igor Juricevic. "Foreshortening, Convergence and Drawings from a Blind Adult." *Perception* 35, no. 6 (2006): 847–51.

National Parks Service. *All In! Accessibility in the National Park Service, Five-Year Strategic Plan.* Washington, DC: National Parks Service, 2015.

———. *Director's Order 16A.* Washington, DC: National Parks Service, 1999.

———. *Director's Order #42.* Washington, DC: National Parks Service, 2000.

———. *The National Parks Service Special Directive 83-3.* Washington, DC: National Parks Service, 1983.

Pavlov, Ivan. *Conditioned Reflexes.* Mineola, NY: Dover Publications, 1927.

Reiser, Roger, and John Dempsey, *Trends and Issues in Instructional Design and Technology.* London: Pearson, 2011.

Saettler, Paul. *A History of Instructional Technology.* New York: McGraw-Hill, 1968.

Skinner, Buhurus. *Beyond Freedom and Dignity.* New York: Bantam Books, 1972.

Thorndike, Edward. "Animal Intelligence: An Experimental Study of the Associative Processes in Animals." *Psychological Monographs: General and Applied* 2, no. 4 (1898): i–109.

United Nations. *Enable: Rights and Dignity of Persons with Disability.* Geneva, Switzerland: United Nations, 2006.

Web Resources

"About Maine." State of Maine, accessed December 25, 2020. https://www.maine.gov/portal/about_me/index.html.

"About Utah." State of Utah, accessed December 25, 2020. https://www.utah.gov/about/.

"About Wyoming." State of Wyoming, accessed December 25, 2020. http://www.wyo.gov/about-wyoming.

"Acadia National Park, Maine." National Parks Service, accessed December 25, 2020. https://www.nps.gov/acad/index.htm.

"Alaska Information." State of Alaska, accessed December 25, 2020. http://alaska.gov/kids/learn/information.htm.

"California History Section." State of California Library, accessed December 25, 2020. https://www.library.ca.gov/california-history/.

"The Climate of Alaska." Weather Atlas, accessed December 25, 2020. https://www.weather-us.com/en/Alaska-usa-climate#climate_text_1.

"The Climate of Arizona." Weather Atlas, accessed December 25, 2020. https://www.weather-us.com/en/arizona-usa-climate#climate_text_1.

"The Climate of California." Weather Atlas, accessed December 25, 2020. https://www.weather-us.com/en/california-usa-climate#climate_text_1.

"The Climate of Colorado." Weather Atlas, accessed December 25, 2020. https://www.weather-us.com/en/colorado-usa-climate#climate_text_1.

"The Climate of Florida." Weather Atlas, accessed December 25, 2020. https://www.weather-us.com/en/florida-usa-climate#climate_text_1.

"The Climate of Maine." Weather Atlas, accessed December 25, 2020. https://www.weather-us.com/en/maine-usa-climate#climate_text_1.

"The Climate of Pennsylvania." Weather Atlas, accessed December 25, 2020. https://www.weather-us.com/en/pennsylvania-usa-climate#climate_text_1.

"The Climate of Utah." Weather Atlas, accessed December 25, 2020. https://www.weather-us.com/en/utah-usa-climate#climate_text_1.

"The Climate of Washington." Weather Atlas, accessed December 25, 2020. https://www.weather-us.com/en/washington-usa-climate#climate_text_1.

"The Climate of Wyoming." Weather Atlas, accessed December 25, 2020. https://www.weather-us.com/en/wyoming-usa-climate#climate_text_1.

"Colorado Facts and History." State of Colorado, accessed December 25, 2020. https://www.colorado.gov/pacific/archives/ColoradoFacts.

"Denali National Park, Alaska." National Parks Service, accessed December 25, 2020. https://www.nps.gov/dena/index.htm.

"Discover Arizona." State of Arizona, accessed December 25, 2020. https://az.gov/discover.

"Everglades National Park." UNESCO, accessed December 25, 2020. https://whc.unesco.org/en/list/76/.

"Everglades National Park, Florida." National Parks Service, accessed December 25, 2020. https://www.nps.gov/ever/index.htm.

"Gettysburg National Military Park, Pennsylvania." National Parks Service, accessed December 25, 2020. https://www.nps.gov/gett/index.htm.

"Grand Canyon National Park." UNESCO, accessed December 25 2020. https://whc.unesco.org/en/list/75/.

"Grand Canyon National Park, Arizona." National Parks Service, accessed December 25, 2020. https://www.nps.gov/grca/index.htm.

"Olympic National Park, Washington." National Parks Service, accessed December 25, 2020. https://www.nps.gov/olym/index.htm.

"Pennsylvania Facts & History." Visit Pennsylvania, accessed December 25, 2020. https://www.visitpa.com/facts-and-history.

"Rocky Mountain National Park, Colorado." National Parks Service, accessed December 25, 2020. https://www.nps.gov/romo/index.htm.

"Washington." Visit USA, accessed December 25, 2020. https://www.visittheusa.co.uk/state/washington.

"Weird, Wonderful Facts About Florida." Visit Florida, accessed December 25, 2020. https://www.visitflorida.com/en-us/travel-ideas/10-florida-facts.html.

"Yellowstone National Park, Wyoming." National Parks Service, accessed December 25, 2020. https://www.nps.gov/yell/index.htm.

"Yosemite National Park, California." National Parks Service, accessed December 25, 2020. https://www.nps.gov/yose/index.htm.

"Zion National Park, Utah." National Parks Service, accessed December 25, 2020. https://www.nps.gov/zion/index.htm.

INDEX

accessible bathroom. *See* bathroom
accessible technology, 21, 22, 23, 24, 46, 49–62
alt text, 9
American Sign Language. *See* sign language
ASL. *See* sign language
assistive technology. *See* accessible technology
audio description, 11, 36, 46, 77, 93, 122, 138, 181, 187, 205, 214, 221, 228n13
autism, 11, 56, 202

bathroom, 10, 86, 88, 89, 90, 91, 103, 104, 107, 108, 119, 120, 121, 147, 149, 151, 152, 164, 165, 166, 167, 169, 181, 183, 184, 195, 196, 198, 199, 201, 218, 219, 220, 221
Braille, 2, 4, 6, 9, 11, 32, 42, 57–58, 78, 93, 94, 103, 104, 123, 133, 148, 171, 187, 223, 229n17
bus, 12, 70, 77, 85, 86, 87, 88, 90, 91, 93, 115, 117, 118, 121, 130, 131, 132, 133, 134, 135, 136, 162, 163, 194, 195, 196, 197, 198, 199, 211, 212, 213, 214, 217, 218, 219, 222, 235n4
bus station. *See* bus

captions, 5, 9, 11, 42, 46, 47, 92, 94, 103, 104, 109, 133, 148, 167, 180, 181, 198, 202, 217
cell phone. *See* mobile technology
clinic. *See* hospital
closed captions. *See* captions

dementia, 7, 11, 56
disability lift. *See* elevator

elevator, 43, 70, 73, 86, 102, 119, 162, 166, 167, 195

ABOUT THE AUTHOR

Simon J. Hayhoe is the author of eight books on art education and museum access for people with disabilities and is also an educational advisor for the World Health Organization. His current work focuses on inclusive mobile technologies, and he has just completed a project investigating the use of mobile technologies by disabled people in museums and monuments. Hayhoe has also won numerous awards in his field, including a Fulbright Award and a Fellowship of the Metropolitan Museum of Art, and he has presented his work at major museums and colleges in the US, Russia, the UK, Singapore, Belgium, and Italy. Beyond work and writing, Hayhoe lives with his wife and two children, close to where he was born and raised.